AF584414

Around the world with writers, scientists and philosophers

Around the world with writers scientists and philosophers

Michel Serres

Translated from the French by Gila Walker

GAZEBO BOOKS SUMMER HILL 2022

Gazebo Books
PO Box 375
Summer Hill
New South Wales 2130
Australia
gazebobooks.com.au

Originally published in French as *Ecrivains, savants et philosophes font le tour du monde* by Michel Serres

First published in English translation by Gazebo Books, 2022

National Library of Australia
Cataloguing-in-Publication Entry
Author: Serres, Michel, 1930-2019.
Around the world with writers, scientists and philosophers
First edition
ISBN 978 0 6454648 9 4 (paperback)

Cover and interior design by Mountains Brown Press.
Cover photograph: Creative Commons CC BY– MRAH/KMKG.

For Audrey, Béatrice and Jennifer, the Three Graces

And Emmanuel, their Apollo

Three tours of the world

As a young man, I'd decided, insanely, that a philosopher's life had to start with three impossible necessities, three tours to complete. Before attaining a wisdom postponed to some faraway future, the apprentice must first, by way of preparation, tour the world, or so I thought. He must visit ice floes and the Pacific, see icebergs drifting and whales blowing, cross deserts, climb mountain peaks, experience earthquakes and volcanoes, sail the high seas, brave cyclones, explore islands and continents. In short, soak up the harsh beauty of the planet. Wander. At the outer limits of muscular fatigue, of brief life's short scale and of admirative enthusiasm, no one can possibly see everything. I was left with the melancholy of leafing through maps of the world.

Luckily, a complete tour of sorts did come. Because, by a misfortune, unexpected though long in the making, the world war, the one we are conducting against the world, is confronting today its immanent, tangible, calculable and threatening global power, which compels us, under extreme risk and by force, to sign a Natural Contract of symbiosis. Thus, in an uncanny, surprising and dangerous way, we are completing the millions of years long journey of *Sapiens*, stopped all together before this new integration, before this sum that summons us. This does not mean that I've seen and learnt everything about our blue planet, not by a long shot, but rather that I am, in the company of all, living through an experience that gives us access to its totality. The sum total of our interventions ended up rousing and revealing the whole of the world, in reality a Hand, no longer invisible and transcendent like that of the market, but immanent and threatening. We thought we were manipulating the world, when it has ended up manipulating us.

Next, the apprentice must complete a tour of knowledge. This second journey summons another impossible necessity. Whereupon, despairing but patient, the aforesaid aspirer absorbs mathematics and the related hard sciences, from cosmology to biochemistry, plus the human, social and political sciences. Given that the centre of this circular tour of the encyclopaedia is everywhere and its circumference nowhere, the apprentice, well-intentioned though he may be, loses sight of the big picture.

Now, by an inconceivable stroke of luck and unexpected good fortune, the Great Story, at life's end, completes this interminable circuit several times. The cycle of four books beginning with *Hominescence* goes over this extensively. By this mapping of duration, by this chronological world map, the cognitive journey ends or integrates a project that the prior global journey could not bodily complete, but that today summons the force of things. This does not mean that I finally know everything, and in detail, not by a long shot, but rather that I have available to me, like everyone else, through this temporally deployed totality, an infinite number of easy gateways to all possible knowledge.

My programme of preparation for philosophy was to extend these two enchantments by completing a tour of humans. But, again, the many cultures, languages, religions and customs, and mostly the many individuals, each constituting, singly, almost a species, formed an impassable obstacle to my foolhardy courage. Here, there were even fewer possible sums or integrations than in the two preceding projects.

Once again at life's end, destiny gifted me a third stroke of good fortune. Philippe Descola had recently classified human cultures into four archipelagos (*Beyond Nature and Culture*, University of Chicago, 2013). Thus, he came to the rescue of my final folly: I could imagine completing the tour of humans.

So here I am, at long last, ready to become a philosopher.

As a farmer and sailor's child, a *langue d'oc* speaker, conscious of bearing a culture different from the one whose elements I received in high school and universities or from reading the major texts that were taught there, I was often outraged to see the self-same human beings, always from the self-same places, studying certain other human beings. Who ever saw a group of Pyrenean shepherds or Mongolian herdsman flocking to the Collège de France, Cornell or Oxford University to observe the political, sexual and religious mores of the professors and researchers haunting those heights? Some human sciences function in semiconduction. I dreamt of reversing this point of view.

Whether we classify them as poetry, novels, science or philosophy, can we read ancient, medieval, modern or contemporary Western works, for example, as if we were listening to the words of the Kwakiutl or the Inuit, the Achuar or the Dogons? Can we reverse our site to see our own culture as a field of ethnological study? Montesquieu's Parisian asks, 'How can one be Persian?' I dreamt of crying out, How can one write, perceive and think Western? Having lived and thought as a Gascon did not suffice to accomplish this project. This site, narrow as it is, and the knowledge that went with it, limited as it is, didn't provide sufficient footing. What was needed was a point of view as broad as the object to be reversed in the opposite direction.

A point of view, an observation site, the apex of a visual cone, provides an oblique view, on a partial or full-scale object – that's all. Classical theorists called this perspective a scenography, in other words the scene that forms on the section of the visual cone. I saw the culture that we call Western from the small, limited point of view of an Occitan farmer, a singular, narrow, partial scenography – in short, inconsiderable. The aforementioned classification forms, on the world's cultures, what the classical period called an ichnography or a ground plan. God alone, according to Leibniz, can see everything or the world from every point of view at once, since he honours, with his ubiquitous presence, all possible sites, at the same time. He alone can presume to see the thing as it is, integrating the sum of all scenographies. Now the classification is dedicated to this sum, integrates its calculation, groups its relationships: relative universality, says Descola. We can now see all cultures, one by one, from this new site, which I thought inaccessible, save to the omniscient God of the classical period. So why not look at our own? I saw my dream virtually come true.

This book describes that dream.

The four worldviews

Each chapter below cites one of the worldviews drawn from the aforementioned classification, as it is practiced in the tribes of Amazonia, Australia or the Far North. Why not speak instead of religion, given that we are dealing in fact with classifying relationships?

Animism sees the same soul in all beings, each clothed in an original body. *Naturalism*, on the contrary, sees all bodies as made up of the same ingredients (molecules and atoms) whereas souls, gifted with interiority, animate only humans, personally different and varied for cultures and societies; this second worldview tends to characterise the recent West. *Totemism* understands the differences between human beings through those that plant or animal species manifest, and sometimes draws correspondences between a human being and an animal or a plant. *Analogism* regards all that exists as different and struggles to find possible relationships in this disparate disorder.

The tour of the world thus reveals a different map than the physical or political worldmap and partitions it in a new way based on the worldview of a given culture. Instead of five continents delimited by oceans, this classification yields four archipelagos in which geographically remote societies are grouped together. I used this map to move within my culture.

A language with several voices

So I was able to complete my tour of the world without leaving my habitat. Because, long ago and recently still, we Westerners, were and remain animists and totemists. Yes, we formed and still adhere to these worldviews, less other than akin. Surprisingly, could it be that our ancient heritage and contemporary formats fall into the same categories as cultures that ethnology classifies as such? The only effort needed to understand this grouping involves not extending it over the time of history and pretending, like Comte and others, that we were once fetishists, for example, and that progress has led us today to a more accurate worldview, freed of these old mistakes. This type of narrow narrative, usually informed by an ideology that is naïve or, worse, vindictive toward its predecessors, projects back over time and in the present that it brings to a close all the *centrisms* that it condemns in space.

Like this newly pieced together archipelago, my new portolan chart groups spaces occupied by the works of writers, poets or novelists, historians, philosophers and scientists from all fields, mathematics, biochemistry, religion, theology and so on. The totemist continent, the animist island and so on, combine, in turn, and without notable distinction, all of the populations, thoughts or deeds that our cultures delight in separating. For the first time, I can make a second dream come true, namely, to speak with many voices, to enunciate, in a common language, genres, discourses, practices, theories that we like to think of as different from one another. I enjoy being able to say, in the single utterance of a sentence, kerygma and theorem, novella and poem, history and system. In other words, on the new ethnological map, islands as distant in terrestrial space as Siberia, Central America and Mali become neighbours; according to the book that follows, another map brings regions together that are as foreign in our culture as rites and ballads, numbers and novels.

Like Harlequin with his multi-coloured cloak could become the all-white lunar Pierrot, the new archipelago could spread, then tend toward a sort of continent or sum in varied shades of grey: a *stem.* I'd like this *totipotent* metaphysics to emerge, flexible enough to leave as many choices to free invention and novelty.

Thus, from cells, life is made, differentiated from stem cells in multiple ways.

A short treatise on ahistorical critique

That literary history aspires to explicate or elucidate a work by the economic, social, political, psychological and other conditions of the time is the exact project of publications whose fashionable content reiterates or reflects the surroundings, like a page in a journal. The common events that such historical critique describes enter into the category of necessary conditions: that the author, son of this man or that woman, lives here or there, under given constraints, constitutes necessity; but, to explain the person's work, sufficient conditions, rare enough to remain out of reach, have to be found. Thus this historic enterprise serves mainly to reproduce itself in university curricula.

The history of science isn't exempt from a similar doubt. It often gives way to dramaturgies in the course of which the succession of paradigms or *epistemes*, interspersed with interruptions, makes for exciting storytelling, theatrical to be sure, but it is also a matter of truth, with conditions as necessary as above. For history brims over with such quantities of facts that any chain of events can be evidenced; all one has to do is choose, sort, keep some and disregard others for the chain in question to appear veracious. Given that the enterprise is constantly possible, the historian is never mistaken. Always being right isn't really good news, since any other account could be equally true, any other telling would meet with equal success. Laughable?

Not really. Be it in music, painting, literature or science, when a discovery arises, when an inventor appears whose intuition changes the worldview, then alterity strikes down the mimetism like a lightning bolt. Originality doesn't disturb in the least the sheep that follow the contemporary, whose conditions seem so necessary to all that they cannot see it materialise. The creator is just another among the many who are alike, predictable and hence incapable of perceiving the unexpected, the hidden, since he brings an elsewhere here and the untimely now. To shield themselves from the lightning that risks burning them, the many who are alike, gird themselves against this other whom they refuse to recognise or whom they exclude if they risk glimpsing him. And when this other makes common history obsolete, how could you expect this same history to explain it?

Looking outside time and elsewhere is, quite simply, a voyage through space, a tour of the world of cultures. The results of taking this journey while remaining in one place were deeply satisfying. I do not claim that they are all and always true, but I would rather they be falsified by those who are more refined than I.

Adorned with feathers in the midst of a crowd of uniform wigs, do our decisive fathers, do our geniuses of the day, hunt alone in compact forests?

Our totemist lineage

Three definitions of totemism. The first, the popular one, associates a man or a group with a given animal, plant or even a quality. And so a comic book will call a native American character Bold Eagle, and the French transit authority, absurdly, calls a road information system Bison Futé (literally a 'savvy buffalo'). I confess with no shame that as a teenager the boy scouts assigned me the personal totem *Enthusiastic Fox*, which was something of an honour for me since I venerate this mammal and am fond of personal gods. But I also had a group totem: I was a Fox who belonged for many years to the Tigers patrol. At least both were, without contradiction, carnivorous, quadruped mammals.

The second definition, more collective, apparently more scientific too, derives from Lévi-Strauss's work. His *Totemism* elucidates a logic in which the classifying effort uses easily observable differences between plant and animal species – who does not see how different eagles and wolves are? – to demonstrate analogous discontinuities between groups, or even tribes.

In classifying the 'ontologies' of the planet in four categories that serve as chapters of his book, Philippe Descola cites these two definitions of totemism, one more individual, the other more social, and emphasises the resemblance of intimacies as much as of bodies, of all living things. Consequently he carves out an archipelago on the worldmap that runs from the Aboriginal peoples of Australia to the Amerindians of high latitudes as well as of the Amazon. I will, in my turn, try to delineate a few totemist islands in our own usages and in our institutions, in our literature and among our scientists.

Our wolf totem

In La Fontaine's *Fables*, it is the Fox who speaks most often (what an honour for my totem!) followed closely by King Lion. The Wolf comes third.

But the bloody fable that the French can still readily recite tells of the cruelty of the wolf who carries the lamb off to the woods and wolfs him down 'without any other why or wherefore'. Our parents inculcated us with a terror of the wolf. It haunted our lives, our nights and the stories we were told. Elsewhere, I have shown how, unlike our *Fables*, we, our shepherds, our dogs, our parents and our teachers readily made it our victim. Having been turned into a scapegoat, La Fontaine's wolf was merely taking his revenge, in a nearly legitimate way, and not before pronouncing an eloquent speech in his own defence. In sparer terms, only Vigny shows insight in celebrating *La Mort du Loup* (*The Death of the Wolf*). He turns the animal into a sublime stoic.

Terror nonetheless: in the Landes forest, George Sand suffered from insomnia due to anxiety, while her husband, Baron Dudevand, slept like a log despite the howling wind that shook the woods facing their windows. No doubt like the rest of us, she must have read La Fontaine, whereas he, of hunting stock, archaic in comparison with his modern companion, felt an old familiarity, an ancient lupine complicity. The couple divorced: she, all tillage and pasturage;

he, the hunter-gatherer; she, post-Neolithic; he, still tangled in totems; thousands of years separated them; they did not live in the same anthropological culture. How could a young feminist bear to be with an archaic man of the woods? In rereading this episode in *Story of My Life: The Autobiography of George Sand*, I saw France more differentiated still in its regions, cultures, and languages than in my youth; so I can easily imagine George Sand, as a mediocre anthropologist from the province of Berry, incapable of understanding the behaviour of a savage from the Landes living his life in the company of wolves. Who would Mowgli marry?

Just think how many hamlets and villages, in this so very differentiated France, and how many families and people bear the name Louviers, La Louvière, Loupiac or some other variation on the root *loup* ('wolf'), still evidencing this recent antiquity? Yes, we lived with the wolves, feared them, hunted them, respected them; they gave us the dog, our best friend. La Fontaine, he again, conveys, albeit not explicitly but better than anyone, how domestication came about, no doubt through hunger and the shared hunt. I will return to this below.

Wolves also taught us how to teach our children. Romulus and Remus were suckled by a wolf; *lupa*, so they say, also referred to the prostitute, who thereby had a totem of her own! The Lyceum of Athens and the many *lycées* in France remind us, as did Tite-Live or *The Jungle Book*, of the ingenious pedagogy, known to hunters and ethologists alike, involved in organising the breeding and hunting preparations in the packs. As everyone knows, *lycée* is the French translation of the Greek for wolf. France conceived of its little ones as *lycéens*, just as Baden-Powell, South African colonialist, an admirer of Kipling (a pseudo-Hindu for his part), saw his as wolf cubs. Teaching made me, like many of my fellow *lycéens* and wolf-cubs, a totemised Wolf twice over. This then is my third carnivorous, quadruped mammal.

After a few innocuous trials, the French national administration still crowns some adolescents with a *bacca lauri*, a 'laurel berry', translated in the vernacular to *baccalauréat*, proof that it classifies its young boys and girls by way of another totem, this one floral. When Pliny the Elder classifies certain plants, adding social and honourable functions to the virtues we call objective, like the oak leaves adorning the head of the military strategist, we laugh, without understanding his totemism, to be sure, but also ignoring our own, which informs our language still today.

Wolves also taught us the dominance of Akela, presiding from his rock over council meetings, like our old masters in the Louvre. Which wolves haunted this den of kings? Or did the kings behave, there, like sons of the she-wolf (*louve*)? Our culture, historical and political, runs from the Lycée to the Louvre. Do we ever leave the wolves behind? And how many nightmares have us turning into lycanthropes, or werewolves? Inherited from eras when we, hunter-gatherers, roamed the Earth, these metamorphoses haunt us still. Before rereading Ovid or Apuleius, we wake up as wolf-children. No, the *Wolf Totem* does not belong only to the Mongolian steppe, as told by Jiang Rong, for it is an integral part of our heritage or at least it has left legible traces on our places and their names, our stories, our customs, our habits and our dreams. Without these active and dark gaps in our memories, would the adventure of Victor of Aveyron or the recent return of packs in the Alps have triggered such a strong emotional reaction?

Francis of Assisi, the troubadour, whose love for flowers and birds reconnects with the pagan religions still rooted in the local and European peasantry of his day, hastens, once again, to Gubbio, to the wolf. *Il Poverello*, for whom I've had nothing but admiration and love all my life, goes into its lair, speaks to the mute animal and makes it promise to stop its cruelties. In return, the visitor pledges to feed it. Re-enacting the domestication, Francis foresees the symbiosis. Love and hatred, hostility or hospitality, the fraternity of our species with *Canis lupus* does not cease. Saint Francis, the historians say, converted the still pagan peasant world to Christianity, which had been confined to cities until then. He did so by presenting them with a religion that was totemist here, animist there, like theirs. Christian-pagan, Saint Francis enhanced one religion with another. In this respect too, I follow him.

We are still totemists, unwittingly, in many of our

customs and institutions. In love and close to their pets, how many children – and adults flanked by their Dog totem – have remained so …

… as have many of the texts of our literature … Totemism's power of classification explodes in La Fontaine's *Fables*, where the animals and plants, abundantly present, show, by hiding them, the presence, at least virtual, of humans. Most of the titles or subjects oppose two species: 'The Donkey and the Dog', 'The Oak and the Reed', 'The Two Friends' and so on. The differential gap, easily recognisable between the animals or the plants, brings order, as we've seen, amongst the foolish and the gentle, the violent and the weak, the humble and the great – in short, amongst characters, social groups or classes.

The socio-political interpretation of the *Fables* splits its totemist structure, as it concentrates solely on humans – who are barely evoked, except for the rare miller, cobbler, financier or mogul king – whilst disregarding the animals and plants, Lion or Pumpkin, Oak or Wolf, despite their superabundant presence. Thus it reduces to current history a gigantic duration whose temporal thickness goes back to even before the written word. Because, before the Latin *Phaedra*, or the Greek Aesop, before even Ahiqar, whose Story, in Aramaic which Aesop no doubt plagiarised, was a huge success in the Assyrian-Babylonian world in around the 7th to 5th centuries BCE, fables of this kind, in oral form, ran rampant in the countryside. Thus it reduces, to the narrow and supposedly 'cultivated' surrounding space from which 'nature' is already receding, traditions scattered all over the world and received long ago and recently still, even here, at least in and through rustic life, at least in and through fables, but forgotten for all time by scholars in the cities. Our literary history never sees the lion, wolf or donkey, but always the king, lord and peasant. Politics, social classes, law, morality and so on are supposed never to have varied over the millennia, neither from Mogul to Paris, from Assyria to Greece, from Rome to France, nor from the Neolithic to computers. And as a result, the *Fables*, wide, long and deep, disappear under barely even a tenth of their short and flat sociopolitical morality.

For a long time, I sought a plan or some order in these texts: foolish project. All you have to do is see them deploying the totems – Wolf, Acorn or Frog – to understand that the *Fables* amount to classification. They totemise social chaos precisely for the purpose of bringing the obvious order or classification of the living to it. Recourse to the more or less visible relief of species seems to be the best way to understand the divisions and distinctions of human relations. The collective is ranked in the way animals eat each other. Thus the order of the *Fables* reproduces that of the living. This is totemism, Lévi-Strauss style.

Conversely, animals and plants are absent in La Bruyère's *Caractères*. I continue with Theophrastus's characters, he says, and start mine through the translation of his. What is the reason for this procession? It is less a matter of a Modern imitating an Ancient, and less of the Quarrel, mimetic and *picrocholin*, than of going back to an undoubtedly archaic state, one whose presence persists, albeit hidden.

For Theophrastus, disciple of and successor to Aristotle, almost a precursor in botany, classified the animals and their various parts. When La Bruyère mentions, in passing, the works of his model that history preserved, he cites his treatises on natural history, plants, fish, rocks and honey, among others. How did Theophrastus go from this first order, that of the natural world, to the second, that of the social world, which sought a semblance of reason in his *On Moral Characters*? How did Aristotle, before him and in a similar way, go from the study of animals to that of the Constitution and institutions of Athens? How does the zoologist and botanist turn away from plants and animals to classify individuals and groups? By untying the totemist device that binds them? Indeed, it sufficed to consider, each separately, the two differentiated elements or sets of the bond that totemism creates.

Many cultures find it convenient to draw a parallel between the differences between living species, which seem obvious, and those that distinguish people, groups or individuals. The elaboration of this connection, the opening of this passage, is what ethnologists call totemism. The writings of Aristotle and those of his disciple, inasmuch as they open onto the social sciences, seem to split this device in two, to yield, on the one hand, natural history, in a still impure state, and, on the other, a still specific knowledge of institutions or characters. With Theophrastus, in fact, as with his successor, the portraits still mix individuals with species, the Garrulous with Boorishness, the Grumbler with Avarice, etc., as if they both still had difficulty distinguishing the singular from its group. The aforementioned quarrel of the Ancients and the Moderns weighs little compared to this archaic succession. Did La Bruyère suspect this? Does literary history suspect this?

At least our languages themselves recall that the word *Characters* in the title of the work, comes from the Latin *character,* for the iron, turned red hot, used to brand domestic animals, for the most part, sheep, cattle or horses. The Latin comes in turn from the Greek, *kharax*, χάραξ, originally a botanic – or rather a gardening – term, used by Theophrastus in his *On the Causes of Plants*. It refers to an olive branch that has been tapered and sharpened to a point at the tip to be replanted as a cutting; it designates at once the notch and the cutting; it is used thereafter to refer to vine canes, then to the stake, and indicates the palisade made of these branches, thus marked and assembled to surround a community. Does this common practice hide the practice of having an entrenchment, a city or a camp, provided not only with a tall and solid material protection, but also with the symbolic protection, derived from the totem, from the botanical species from which the users drew the stakes? Before indicating traces of writing or grouping the singular and constant behaviours of an individual, the word character signalled the connection proceeding from the work of a human on a plant, both individuals first of all, to be generalised to membership in a group, thereupon protected by the cuts of the self-same plant. Totemism resides as well in the title of the two books, the ancient and the modern.

It comes back through the window of the room where Félicité dies, her stuffed parrot perched on one of the altars where the Corpus Christi day procession stops. Flaubert turns the chapel into a bazaar. The girl's room, her own altar, is also a bazaar where she has accumulated hundreds of souvenirs. Does this *Simple Soul* overturn Catholicism to find other ritual practices alongside it? Which?

Fetishism, to begin with. The clothes, the remains of those she knew, these are the detailed objects onto which Félicité regressively fixes her affect, in Freudian terms. But, chosen among this bric-à-brac, the parrot, alive at first, then stuffed, shifts from the affective to the religious. The servant received it as a gift from a baron, ex-consul in America, who had brought it back from there, along with the Black servant. Has an exotic rite left its mark in Normandy? Flaubert as Indian?

Kinless, loveless, fortuneless, wordless, spiritless, repetitive in her language, Félicité does not exist. She becomes aware of herself very late in life, at the top of Ecquemauville, upon seeing the lights of Honfleur, after an accident in which she nearly lost her life and the dead body of the parrot. Does she understand that she differs from others like the parrot, by species? And like him, that she speaks little, repeating what others say? Dead or alive, does the animal give her something of a personal existence? Flaubert, it is said, wrote this story alongside another stuffed parrot, perched on his table, which did not take its glass eyes off of him. Did it play the same role, for him, as Félicité's parrot, suddenly transformed, at death's door, into the Holy Ghost? Does the third person of the Trinity add a trait of totemism to Christianity, or, blowing in an impetuous wind, of animism?

The answer resides in the altar where idols, totems and signs of monotheism are gathered. This is the scale model of the immense mix found in *The Temptation of Saint Anthony* which does with religion what *Bouvard and Pécuchet* does with science. By saddling his two unforgettable autodidacts, one with the name of a bovine, Bouvard – *bos, bov-* 'ox' – in echo to Bovary, and the other with the name of the herd, Pécuchet – *pecus, pecoris* – Flaubert totemises them, giving them the forehead of the bull and the intelligence of the ruminant. The first of his *Three Tales* unfolds like a genealogy of totemism. It explains how we can conceive of our own difference with the help of a species with which we identify, body and soul. As for the hero of the second tale, Saint Julian the Hospitalier, at once hunter and emperor, he dominates animal species and human populations, as if, connected through him, they existed in parallel, each people corresponding to a species.

Hérodias, the last of the three, organises a feast of dishes, drinks and religions, which ends with a sacrifice, the beheading of John the Baptist. In this scale-model feast, as much as in the giant, mad panorama depicted in *The Temptation of Saint Anthony*, Flaubert, fascinated by the religious, seeks to create a kind of *stem* from which visions of the world and religions would come one by one. Far from historicising them, as they are in *La Légende des siècles*, he blends them into a compact paste or rather associates, juxtaposes, relates them like in a chapel, a museum or a bazaar. Likewise, Bouvard and Pécuchet accumulate disparate knowledge, higgledy-piggledy ... another feast, another temptation, a museum, a bazaar, a collection ... another cognitive parallel of the identified stem. Just as this book, in conclusion, will rediscover these stems, these collages will come back in droves when it is time to tackle the third ontology: the analogical.

The origin of natural sciences

It is barely a step from Bouvard and Pécuchet's comic knowledge to veridical, veritable knowledge. The totemism of Lévi-Strauss erupts, for instance, at the memory of one of those anecdotes with which legend or veracity embellishes the history of sciences. A famous naturalist, his name (Jussieu?) doesn't matter, was presenting a specimen of a rare species in an amphitheatre in the Jardin des Plantes, formerly known as the Jardin du Roi. He asked his audience to identify the animal or plant. Ignorant or taken aback, the attendees were silent. Then the door at the back of the room opened violently and in rushed a man, out of breath, his overcoat billowing behind him. He courteously removed his hat, immediately recognised the living organism and, exulting over its beauty, he named it twice, first by its vernacular and then by its scientific Latin name. Oh! the professor exclaimed, if you succeeded in answering my question you must be Monsieur de Linné. The stranger bowed and smiled: I've just come from Stockholm.

Disprove this story, if you will, and its academic signification bursts forth ever more clearly: specialists in the sciences recognise their own differences based on the difference of species … or objects of their knowledge … just as men and women do in the totemist tribes that ethnologists describe. Whereas the so-called 'naturals' are named after certain animals, our scientists call them by the name of the first amongst them, thus distinguished, who claimed to have found, or rather described them.

Ethnologists see this '*pensée sauvage*', this 'wild thought', as classifying; in a complementary or symmetrical manner, who doesn't see the scientists who classify animals and plants as totemists? In his *Philosophie botanique* (1751), Linné himself compares his own classification, having become classic if I dare say – class, order, genus, species – with others that order men: armies – legion, cohort (but who recalls that the said co-hort completes the garden, *hortus*?), maniple ...– political or territorial divisions – kingdom, province, parish ... – and even philosophical concepts – genus, species, individual. The term class itself goes back to the Latin *classis*, that distinguishes, among the people, those citizens who can be called to arms. The master of nomenclature was concerned, as we see, with ordering living organisms no differently than men.

Conversely, many classifications – those of Ampère, Bentham or Comte for the sciences, of Boissier de Sauvages for diseases, or even of Propp for narratives, and others for museology, or even for emotions – intentionally draw inspiration from classifications in botany and zoology. What is called *natural* history never ceases to accompany history in the broadest sense, politics, social organisation, human accomplishments, in short, what we call *culture*. Everyone knows this parallel; how is it that no one has given it its true name? For this relationship has a name but one hidden out of fearfulness. Let us not hesitate to use it: that totemism classifies, we know, ethnologists have taught us so; but we hide its reflection in a mirror, where I see classifications of all sorts and their authors as totemists.

Who nowadays does not see the sociologists of science at the pinnacle of this totemist tribe? If the above-mentioned Aboriginal peoples of Australia of this rite classify plants or animals based on their own distinctions or, conversely, draw distinctions between their fellow humans based on living species, sociologists, for their part, delight in projecting onto the whole of nature, and onto global knowledge, the distinctions and classes endured or willed by those who deal with them. This generalised fetishist or totemist gesture earns them the honourable altar at the summit of the hierarchy.

This was the way philosophers proceeded and still do, be it in ancient Greece, in the Middle Ages or, more recently, in the Anglo-Saxon analytic movement: three instances associated with schools or the University. The rarefied and sophisticated multiplicity of their distinctions scholastically mimes the very classes of their teaching, dispute, research and career environments. Approaching concepts or theories like 'wild thought' approaches quadrupeds and birds, they classify and draw distinctions between them with marvellous finesse, unparalleled rigour and, at the same time and no doubt for this purpose, classify and draw attention to themselves. Any newly distinct theory announces over time its author's differentiated genius. How delightful that the most purportedly evolved human beings behave and think like those who are thought to be archaic. I find myself walking on campus like Tintin on a reservation for Arumbayas; but didn't Tintin himself drag Snowy, his totem, behind him?

Isn't classification as much the field of choice for philosophers as it is for sociologists? Doesn't the overabundant output of classes of thought generated by discussions about natural kinds excellently reproduce their own? Can't realists, idealists, pragmatists, nominalists, essentialists and others be arranged on a classification tree, as old as the tree of Porphyry, that resembles the one where all genera and all species to be classified are arranged? Doesn't the fact that the classifiers classify themselves just as they classify their objects, whatever they may be, or that they classify the latter based on viewpoints that classify themselves in the same way reveal a totemism that was, is and will be powerfully active yesterday, today and tomorrow? Ironically, this book itself plays this game.

The -isms of philosophy branch out from it. And enable the debate that enables, in its turn, the classifying. The constant praise that philosophers lavish on the cognitive virtues of opposition, discussion and polemics, shows that the classification – returning to the original Latin *classis*, referring to the arrangement of legions in battle lines – enables them to continue the war by other means, in heated amphitheatres.

So let all see, like Rousseau, botany as peaceful. We ought to laugh no more at Pliny the Elder's classes in his *Natural History* where roosters and peacocks are arranged in a second class of birds, itself divided into two genera: those whose song was consulted by haruspices and those whose flights they consulted; likewise, he associated oak with victorious generals and mistletoe with Gallic druids. This text is not as interesting for a Latinist or a historian of science as it is for an ethnologist who recognises there, unmistakably, an ancestor of our own totemisms.

Better yet, at the end of *L'Herbier des philosophes* (Le Seuil, 2008), Jean-Marc Drouin composes an imaginary collection, summarising his subject through a flowering. He garnishes this delicious herbarium with plants that he associates, one by one, with a botanist so creative that his name has gone down in history: the orchid with Darwin, the poppy with Chamisso, the orange tree with Humboldt and Bonpland, the strawberry plant with Tournefort, the veronica with Linné, the bean with Comte, with its cotyledons, the rose with Candolle, not to mention the Arabidopsis, which he associates with contemporary scientists. Is this some sort of distribution of awards? No, the last chapter answers, in fact and at last, the title of the book is presented in a candidly exact way: the true philosopher of this *Herbier*, the authentic philosopher of life sciences draws a parallel between the differences amongst botanical species and those that distinguish the people that study them; a sterling list of the witches dominating the totemist tribe: to each his flower, to each his totem.

From the archaic era, marked by Pliny or Theophrastus, to the publication of this delicious recent book, can we still imagine that these authors, eminent scientists or learned historians, all Western-style experts in natural history, really separate two distinct spheres, as they are distinguished by conventional modern ideology: nature and culture?

And what if pharmacology had, once and always, emerged from a practice associated with this totemism?

Who, in France at least, has forgotten Gaston Bachelard, whose work cuts the objective lucidity of science off from the intimate dreams of poets? Let no one enter here who hasn't left his dreams at the threshold! But then what to make of witches, with their sabbaths in clearings at night, in which Michelet, not as blind as many, blindly sees the origin of natural sciences and their medicinal applications? Satan, women, nature and science, here are the four outcasts of history and culture grouped together by him, and there they are together condemned to witchcraft trials. On what charges and by what right?

These Michelet-style Middle Ages reflect an otherwise longer and deeper anamnesis. Ancient

Greek science itself emerged in trials similar to the witch trials; Socrates, at his trial, mentions Anaxagoros as being among the countless legal victims of this emerging knowledge. Originating in what could not yet be called human sciences or political activism, the main accusations made against them was that by observing plants, animals or stars these men were not engaged in or occupied with civic affairs. To put it succinctly, in modern terms, by focusing on nature, they were forsaking culture. As if the people of the city, otherwise known as citizens, should be interested in the city, not in the world.

Thus society defended the exclusivity of society, politics the exclusivity of politics and law the exclusivity of law; media and sociology would later defend theirs. Culture always defends the exclusivity of culture. Bachelard does the same for science. The world and men are not to be coupled. *The Natural Contract* was met with the same contempt for the same reason: it had, the accusation was, forgotten the city.

Thus several tribunals – Greek, medieval, ecclesiastic, university – would continue to exclude any relationship to nature, any gesture, thought, attempt that could, closely or remotely, resemble totemism, animism or analogism, to borrow Descola's terminology. By what justice, by what right did these diverse and yet unitary juries draw their constant sentences? It matters little to me to accuse, in my turn, some guilty party, so I don't give a fig about answering this question. Seeking for the sake of finding is more worthwhile than judging.

As a result, our sciences were born, no doubt, one by one and little by little, from one of those forgotten or abandoned worldviews. We remain blind to the question of the emergence of the sciences, because a virtual and trans-historical trial is always lurking around us. You must not join the witch in the clearing. But, conversely, one finds reason not to make a critical judgment, not to take a seat on a tribunal. Critique ruins invention. Masters and professors teach critique to young people, no doubt out of their impotence to invent, but mainly because they are panicked at the thought of invention shaking up all order and all formats.

These witch trials thus revived in the Middle Ages the many ongoing trials of the likes of Anaxagoros, Socrates or Zenon in Greek Antiquity, and they quite simply announced Galileo's, who was nearly the last on the list – or maybe the first of the Moderns – and thereafter the cases brought by fundamentalists against Darwin or against *l'élan vital*, plus those conducted, from the inside, by established science, which continues to put its inventors to death. Out of hatred or fear of 'wild thought'?

And Michelet, whom I join in the forest, enthusiastically describes the attraction of his beloved witch to botany, to calming, soporific or toxic plants; the sympathy, the enchanted fascination of this *medicinal Medea*, healer and murderer, for the solanaceæ or the comforters – here, he cites Pouchet, another sorcerer, and adversary of Pasteur – for the bittersweet, whose honey calms and kills, and for belladonna, *bella dona* ... *Witches' herbs,* composing an herbarium from which other names of totems can be drawn. *The Devil a Physician, Charms and Philtres* ... such is the totemic origin of pharmacology.

The wizard of his witches, the excellent historian of science, Michelet generalises their gesture and doubles his colossal historical output with five books of natural history, strange, short, incisive, instructive and striking. What worldview was he looking to join? Totemism, for sure; animism, perhaps; at any rate, the crossbridge of the *The Troubadour of Knowledge.* I don't think he ever yielded in his writing about kings, princes, and their battles and politics to the outpourings of lyricism that he addressed to 'nature', wild and wooded, and to its companion, the original witch, dark and beautiful. Isn't it paradoxical, and hence significant, that one of the leading historians of our culture venerates, celebrates and prays almost like a priest to the sea (*La Mer*), the bird (*L'Oiseau*), the insect (*L'Insecte*) and the mountain (*La Montagne*), connecting them to the woman (*La Femme*)? Did this nascent knowledge of nature seek to totemise it?

Michelet's contemporary, Auguste Comte, a classifier of the sciences, their origins, historical periods, and the calendar, an extreme classifier in his very style, also ended his life with the religion of the planet, named by him the 'Great Fetish'.

These wise men, clear-sighted at life's end about the origin of their science, are deemed mad by the blind. No one ever reads more than half of Comte or of Schrödinger's *What's Life*.

Through its subtle endeavour of classification, totemism spawned our natural sciences; pharmacology was born, similarly, from a practice close to this origin, in the clearings haunted by the Witch. Is the same true of domestication? After living close to the fox, the tiger and the wolf, since I bore their name, how could I not domesticate at least one? All that was needed was to bring it into the house. Who would have been the host, in that case?

La Fontaine, him again, describes this event. *Canis lupus*, the wild, meets *Canis latrans*, already living on a farm. The slight difference between them comes from this domestication, older, it seems, than all others, so old that between the two animals, diverse in species though they be, flows a continuity. Having become wild again, the brown mastiff swiftly identifies with the real wolf who, conversely, becomes close enough to humans to teach them hunting and strategies of education, as we can read in Livy, in *Panchatantra* or in *The Jungle Book*, and as we can experience in the Mongolian steppe, at the Louvre or in the lycée. Here is a single animal with two heads, like a fetish of sorts. *The Wolf and the Hound* presents this cross-fade. As if one and the same species, untamed-tamed, were speaking to itself, from an immemorial past to an ever-present present. As if domestication itself took place, had taken place, continued to take place along the fetishist, totemist bond that united the wolf and the dog.

The fable firstly exaggerates their differences. In body and space. Whereas the poor wretch is so starved there is nothing left but skin on his bones, the other is fat, bulging with muscles, and bursting with strength and beauty; no fight is possible between the watchdog, stable and strong, and the wanderer, roaming astray (*fourvoyé*), humbled by frailty. Battle, dialogue. Words replace combat. The Hound tells the Wolf about the advantages of domestication, where the hunt is reversed: all he has to do now is chase away beggars, bark at the weak instead of fighting the strong. Buffon compares the ears of wild animals, always pricked up, on the lookout, alert, muscles quivering at the slightest signal, to the drooping, limp auricles of domesticated dogs, relieved of worries and of hearing. *Fiasco*: the payment of protection.

The difference in wolf-dog species coincides with the spatial distance of house-forest, interior-exterior, for the churls with sticks, the beggars, the poor wretches, they too wander astray (*se fourvoient*); the wolves, wild as they are, make their way outside, on pathways in the woods, where the word *four-voyé*, *hors-voyé*, 'outside-path' comes from. The species are distributed and differentiated by their occupation of space: there and out-there (*là* and *horla*). As a result, the opposition between the one that runs off and the one that, attached by the neck, stays put, between the sedentary and the nomad, between the wild and the tame, I was about to say between 'nature' and 'culture', traces a continuous path, in the space thus opened, from the stray (*fourvoyé*), faraway, to the guard, nearby, whose leash and collar measure the narrowness of the gap.

On the path thereby traced, not without some distance, not without a good many obstacles, but that totemism ensures is without interruption, domestication emerges as an entry to the house of a host, *domus*. It begins with totemism, since the analogy between the differences in living species and human differences first brings them together, then builds the very path that comes to an end at the aforesaid house. This path opens up the possibility of finding a host. Along this path, the animal changes, transitioning from the state of predator to that of parasite. Already in *The Eunuch*, Terence described and prepared the transition. In it, Gnato explains how to become a parasite (lines 417-436). As we know, this word measures, precisely, the proximity, *para*, to food, *sitos* in Greek: right alongside food. The leash and collar measure the *para*. The hound advises its mate to leave behind the woods and follow the path to the home of humans where it can immediately, without fighting, find shelter, warmth, food, 'delicacies of every sort […] squab bones and chicken bones' and fond caresses … And most of all to leave behind risk, the harsh struggle to live, and having to 'brave the blade for every crumb'. Thus domestication delineates a journey, a transfer onto this path, defined and framed to begin with by totemism, and on which the living make their way, summoned, baited, swept up by the parasitic state: a fascinating well of attraction. Thus I've often dreamt that life itself had emerged from parasitism.

Fox for the individual, tiger in a team, wolf to stand out by some knowledge ... did I realise that I bore these three totems defined by ethnologists? Around me, do the institutions that characterise our culture, the Louvre or the lycée, see that they sometimes draw their ways and their names from this 'wild thought'? Beyond history, here and there literature draws inspiration from it, discusses, describes and relates it, while philosophers fight around their totems. Better yet, surprising as it may seem, the natural sciences and related technologies, as highly evolved as they are understood to be, seem to emerge from there. If naturalism had separated nature and culture long ago, as we do today, would we know life? How many precise sciences, concerning species, and longstanding practices, pharmacology and domestication, would not even have seen the light of day?

I will try again to show other wild worldviews at the very origin of other exact sciences, and, so as to paint a complete picture, I will revisit, once more, my own life, our familiar customs, our philosophies and our literature.

Soul for all, clothing for each

Inanimate objects, do you have a soul
which sticks to our soul and forces it to love?
Lamartine, *Milly*

My father the sailor did not know how to swim; neither did the dredger nor his apprentice, much less the boatman who unloaded the gravel from the sandpits or the crane operator. My brother and I took advantage of advances in education and spent Thursday afternoons in the lateral canal, not far from the worksite, learning the breaststroke, dangling from jibs on the quay, with a rope around the waist. I took the opportunity to drown, which gave those around me the chance to practice mouth-to-mouth resuscitation. Given that I was born dark and asphyxiated, with three turns in the cord gripping my neck, here I was, born a second time …

My fish age

... in another form: carp, bleak or gudgeon, living in water, under water, in midwater. My brother and I left behind our street urchin ways to become sea urchins. We introduced some neighbourhood rascals into this species, and with them we formed less a gang than a school. Street urchins are called wayward for their ways, what would they have called us: *waterward*?

To the waters we took laughingly, joyfully. We dove under the dredge, explored the green hulls of boats; we waltzed under whirlpools downstream of bridges; we plunged into the cascades of dams. We did not so much wade through the water as inhabit the Garonne more than our homes; we rested in its bed more gently than in our own; we drank in the river that engulfed us. We did not need to make precise or studied gestures, to raise our head or arms out of the water, to swim or let ourselves float. We adapted to the banks and the bottoms, knew the confluents and the counter-currents, the round, sticky pebbles, the sharp rocks, the murky mud and the reeds along the shore, the floods and the low waters of summer. We never went to class or came back from it without first crossing the river, thoroughly surprised to be walking or biking over it.

Pool people practise swimming as a sport, an athletic training, a structured activity. We saw ourselves more as amphibians. Swimming, for us, had the sense that you give something when you feel at ease amid a *milieu*: we swam midjoys. I don't think I'm deceiving myself or my reader when I say that I really had the experience of a gudgeon, having perceived the water, the murky current and the Garonne in person, as something other than things.

This, then, was the first strange-fleshed fetish grafted onto mine – but did the latter precede the former? Child-siren, kid-frog, paedo-potamus, who lost this hydrophilic state as soon as he joined the navy, where he recognised that he was becoming an adult and a father from the fact that no one there knew how to swim. Boats go on the water, not in it. That is when I left behind this primitive animal avatar.

Old as I now am, having long since developed muscles, I'm still wont to gleefully rediscover, in the memory of my skin and my bones, this quivering juvenile trout.

Farm world

Another lost time. That the West in the course the twentieth century abandoned a rurality that the majority of its population practiced until then compels me to say a few obvious things about the past. Rising in the morning, in silence, attentive to the dew, to frost, or to the intense heat, subjected to the vagaries of the seasons, to the regularity of the cycle of the moon, close to their cows and pigs, attuned to fructifications, cereals, grapes, eggs or calves, farmers do not inhabit the same country, do not see or make the same landscape, or even the same space, do not address the same living beings, do not even perceive the same worlds with the same senses as city dwellers, pounding the cobblestones, prisoners of walls, deafened by the din of the street and tongues.

Descended from farmers, I long thought that citizens had invented the nature-culture distinction the better to scorn us as country folk. We ignored this distinction. We beings-in-the-world; they moving in what they called culture; had they stolen from us the culture we practiced, furrowing, sowing and harvesting? As for nature, we lost ourselves in it – body and soul – like sailors at sea. I don't think I'm deceiving myself or my reader in claiming that we knew, vaguely at least, that we were immersed in something immense, pressing, dishevelled, voluminous, whose name we ignored but that had something to do with the frayed edges of clouds, the cry of roosters at night, the roar of the wind in grass; dominated by this shifting and swaying milieu, thrown into its fortunes. They were living in cubes, lines and solids; we in this liquid pitch, bitter and sweet. They seated, dominators, on the built, the regulated, the upright. We, standing, in the unpredictable, the given, the fatal. From rectilinear cities, a Euclidean-type regulated space evaporates into the world; the bouquet of a topological expanse emanated or bifurcated from our life: crowns in forests, barbed ears, feathers and bristles.

When they came to us, for their holidays in August, they found our world so pleasant they felt like they were living in the Arcadia of environmentalists: harvests over, grapes picked, fruit ripe, as yet no ploughing. But no, this ramified milieu in which we swam broke our backs, burnt our skin and hardened it cruelly with calluses, reigning everywhere, aerial, bellowing and clucking, stinking and sweet-smelling, muddy, dusty, disturbing and desirable, heady and soporific ... natural, nascent, mortal. We touched the handlebar of ploughs, the yoke and its leather straps, cobs, grapes, coir, silk, shells, nails and horns ... all hard details, whilst a dishevelled whole – it too hard, but sometimes soft as teat and peach flesh, surfacing like rain and summer smells – submerged these gritty things. Sundry pebbles in a single sea. I hadn't the words then that I have today to convey the profuse distribution of these solid, dense, scattered bodies in a single aerial soul.

Raised in a farming world, I still carry inside me, mute and unknown, the forbidden but immemorial belief in this soul of things, of life and of the world, in a fluid, immense animation whose powerful potential materialises and densifies suddenly, at times, here and there, on crests in the farmyard, on hooves of the stable, in horns aligned in the barn, on the ceps in the nearby wood, in the fields of hay, the orchards of plums, the hawthorn coppices and the black woods of winter. Like my ancestors, I remain a rural animist.

Today's *picrocholin* quarrel of ethology against the Cartesianism of animals-machines disregards farming practices; it also forgets the longstanding theory of French naturalists whose ideas remained in harmony with rural practices, mine as much as theirs, for three centuries. In them, a certain animism, which is frequent, resists the 'naturalism', which is extremely rare; the last chapter of this book will show that in all likelihood the latter has now been reduced to an academic artefact. Like ethnology, ethology goes looking, far far away, among the bonobos or mountain gorillas, for the cultures and customs that my old rurality sustained, right here and for thousands of years, with cows, pigs and hens, and even with ants, foxes and wild boars. Where I find again the farmers from the beginning of my chapter and my life.

So, unlike others, we animist humans live, according to the ethnologists who observe us, as if living, plants and animals, and even objects that some call inanimate, are endowed with the same soul as we are, with the same interiority, the same functions and cultures, intentions and feelings. Only one difference separates us: our bodies, whose thick ball differentiates us in a way that impacts our perception of the other. If mine lets me glimpse the wolf, dog or fish as endowed with human souls, how do these three animals see me? As a man or a fish? This depends on the animist culture, scholars say; it depends on the intensity with which they embody, materialise, weigh down and describe the details of bodies. Some reduce them to an article of clothing – skin, hair or feathers – that each one can freely remove to then put on another. Does my body remember having donned scales or dung-covered shoes.

Whence the ease or, conversely, the difficulty of the metamorphosis, a major operation in these worldviews. Our Western tradition abounds in descriptions of such transformations: Greek and Latin myths, summarised by the cruel Ovid or the amiable Apuleius; La Fontaine and his extreme love of *Donkey Skin*; *Mother Goose Tales*; Cadichon by the enchanting Countess de Ségur; Kafka. Was our past, animist? Is our present? I, at least, will have enjoyed a fluviatile childhood, amidst reeds, and a pagan education, amidst oaks.

Trees in the wind in the last book of the *Fables*

Animism, it is true, cannot do without metamorphoses. If each body is reduced to a piece of clothing, changing clothes provides, in the passing nakedness, a glimpse of the soul, a glimpse of the precise site from which others see themselves and us. We have all sadly seen men and women become beastly, and often. Regressing to the low level of homonisation, they turn into hawks or sharks, silly geese or proud peacocks. In the *Fables,* where these animals, hardened from eating each other, abound, the plant kingdom, gentle from living off of light, is scarce.

Philemon and Baucis loved each other gently; Jupiter and Hermes, who came to them disguised as travellers, turned these two-faithful old people into an oak and a linden. Thus, side by side, with their leaves and crowns, they will never cease from exchanging caresses, for all the eternity of trees. Circe changed Ulysses's companions into swine, boatswains, rascals, and scallywags. La Fontaine turns them into all species of animal. But, following Ovid, he does not transform the two lovers into animals, because heterotrophs kill for food, and hence live on death. Plants and trees, on the other hand, are autotrophs and thereby untainted by this original sin. For this reason, we will say that they are gentle. The wicked, therefore, will become animals, because they kill, whereas the good blossom into Flora and Pomona. Zoologists in hell; loving botanists in the paradise of flowers. Thus, with their frequent animals and scarce plants, the *Fables* separate loving gentleness from hardened evil.

The question is how could two lovers, having become leaves and crowns, exchange caresses without the wind? There is no love, without being moved.

Other trees in the wind in the first book

The Oak and the Reed fight. Behaving like animals? Not really. This masterpiece in which the botanical prevails is less about living beings than about moving forces. For again and again it brings up Aquilo and Zephyrus, the north-wind blast and the gentle west wind, storm and tempest, wrinkles on the face of the water, the fury that uproots trunks or merely bends stalks. The seafaring Joseph Conrad, a much better discerner of breezes than our naïve fabulist, would not have made the mistake of having the stormy fury coming from the north; he gave instead the major title of great ruler of high latitudes to the west wind, towering over the east wind, that minor temporary king. But, wherever they may come from, we all know that we are the playthings of these winds.

Are the two plants actually fighting? Elsewhere, I have compared our old two-player contests, debates or quarrels to decide who is the stronger, the futile fights that oppose men to each other, to a new game with three players, in which the real things of the world intervene. A game that is not as new as all that, since La Fontaine borrowed the scheme from Aesop. *The Oak and the Reed* brings to mind Goya's painting of two adversaries fighting in quicksand. With each blow, their bodies sink further, and this onto death. Sticky and soft, the quicksand prevails here, just as the wind triumphs in the fable. The latter says less about the contest between the two, which is patent, than about the much more formidable contest between three. For which one actually comes out on top in the end? The oak? The reed? Surely one rather than the other, but more significantly the third player that the fable evokes more often, and even from A to Z, from Aquilo to Zephyrus, the player so powerful it crushes the giant that covers and protects everything around it, and so strong it overturns even the most powerful and kills the one that occupies the space near the sky and sinks its roots into the empire of the dead. Even more universal in all the Universe than this cracking upright, the wind wins.

The wood of the oak is hard but does not last; the stalk of the reed, more yielding and gentler, lasts a bit longer, no doubt; another blast and the hard does not last, only the soft does. But even more: here the moving air reigns supreme, with two of its attributes, gentle, when it's a breeze, and hard and furious, when it is the blustery, imperious wind, whose name in Greek is, ἄνεμος, *anemos*, and *anima*, in Latin. Our languages translate the soul. The soul prevails. The spirit? 'The slightest breeze that perchance / *Wrinkles the face* of the water / makes you bow *your head*': the slightest wind, the spirit; the spirit wrinkles the face and bows the head. Would a river have a body, a face unsettled by the breath of a soul? Does the spirit humble the head of the reed? Let us hear how the soul of the world blows. Let us listen to the two bodies: endowed with a soul hard as bark, the Oak cracks and comes crashing down; endowed with a gentle, adaptive soul, the Reed bends and whistles. Unsettling the face of the waters, the storm stains the soul of the trees. La Fontaine ends his first book with a wind of animism. And hadn't he begun it with 'when the winter winds blew free'? He finishes the last one, or nearly, with branches exchanging caresses in the wind of the soul.

'You, your shepherds and your dogs'

Right in the middle of this first book, *The Wolf and the Lamb*, La Fontaine presents the usual conversation of animist hunters – the Achuars of the Amazon and others still – who feel compelled to maintain a kinship, or friendship, with their game. When they are about to make the kill, they speak to them at length, inviting them, indirectly and even hiding their purpose, to surrender to this tragic event. They are, in a way, arguing their case.

In La Fontaine, when the wolf addresses the lamb, saying, 'You, your shepherds and your dogs,' he accurately outlines the chain of the very same kinship to which, through the intermediary of the dog, *canis latrans*, the wolf, *canis lupus*, itself belongs. Keep in mind that the Latin *familia*, the family, included, alongside the adults and children of several generations, farm animals, often living under the same roof. Take, for instance, Perrette, the milkmaid, who lives with her dumb, brutal husband, plus the calves, cow, pig and chickens. As cruel as the wolf, the *paterfamilias* had the right of life and death as much over his children as over his cattle and pigs.

I once gave a very structural analysis of the fable, identifying an ordered structure, in the algebraic sense, unique and multifariously readable: in the flow of the current, upstream, downstream; the high position of the predator, above, below; the genealogy, the engenderment, mother, recent birth; even the birthright, claimed and denied; time, before, after, last year; dominant, dominated ('let not your majesty') – that is, in all respects, *majorant-minorant*.

Whereas the text's formal rigor was nearly totally elucidated in this way, the meaning of this order was lost, because I did not then know how to explain the profound reasoning. Oh what joy, forty years later! Indeed, a truly vital order is played out here, between wolf and lamb, the very process that places the predator before the prey, upstream, that makes it stronger than the prey … And there they are, precisely, both aligned, serialised, belonging to the same family, well known to animist tribes; an order that compels the predator to present a lengthy argument meant to show his future victim the rigorous validity of his hunt.

The other fable in the same first book, *The Wolf and the Hound*, describes, as I have said, the continuous path from the pack to the barn and farmyard, a road that runs thereafter toward the forest, and that is marked, at a given moment in history, by the metamorphosis of domestication, where the purportedly wild wolf nearly changes species. So the one who speaks to the lamb he is about to devour describes this family lineage: you, your shepherds, your dogs, my pack, me. Devouring a relative is not an easy thing to do!

The fable is then completely intelligible since its logical rigor coincides with the meaning of animism: it reproduces the relationship of the hunter to its prey.

If it wasn't practicing a rite that reveals its affiliation with a specific religion, why would the wolf waste so much time indulging in rhetoric as complicated and well-reasoned as an attorney's argument, instead of eating its prey alive, on the spot, and precisely 'without judge or jury'. La Fontaine's, Phaedra's, and Aesop's wolf – and in all likelihood even the older, oral source – simply restates the words of animist hunters who maintain a quasi-kinship, or at least social relations, with the animals which are their food and prey. To the lamb, the wolf gives voice to the predator's reasoning.

If, on the other hand, we were to hunt the wolf, in that case the prey and we the hunters and, in our turn, predators, would we speak to it at such length, along similar lines, before killing it because we think of it as part of the family? In *The Death of the Wolf,* Alfred de Vigny delivers the same argument, as lengthy, as patient, as rigorous, nearly as moralising as La Fontaine's and Phaedra's wolf. Everyone takes this simple speech delivered by an animist hunter to his prey as a lesson in stoic ethics. The wolf could have said to the lamb: 'And then, like I, suffer and die wordlessly.' And Vigny could have added: 'without judge or jury'.

Are we thereby rediscovering the old, and still mysterious, process of domestication? There it is, already embedded in the hunt practiced in this way: welcome home to one who is already part of the family. Totemism, with its bond, frames the two animals. Animism, with its animated dynamism, leads one to the other, in a family-like way. Within the walls of the home, the wolf cub will become a dog. Clothed in thick ears, the common soul of the two bodies sees, from this point of view, what the body arrayed in limp ears sees, from its viewpoint. Symmetrically balanced by *The Death of the Wolf*, *The Wolf and the Lamb* explains *The Wolf and the Hound*. As the first biotechnology, domestication also presupposes this animism.

Proust the Druid: another dating of lost time

In relating fragments of my childhood, as I did at the beginning, I was recalling a truly lost time: that farming world and that river dredging are gone. When Proust published his work, the period that he wrote about existed: the snobbery and the bourgeois salons were still there. Alone, retreating from the advancing macadam, the uneven cobblestones caused the twisting of the narrator's ankles on the teak or the stones of the street to bring him back, suddenly, to a truly lost time. The smooth pavement had replaced the rough, bumpy road.

Because Proust dwells at length on his difficulties falling asleep, we read his memories as returns to the paradise of childhood loves. The taste of the madeleine, the smell of tea, these sensations awaken his memory. We thus naively believe in experiences as crude as Pavlov's experiments in getting his dogs to salivate with a bell that reminds them of food. What is there that is truly lost?

Answer: a time that the author dates expressly and precisely, a few lines before the famous cup of tea passage. 'I feel that there is much to be said for the Celtic belief that the souls of those whom we have lost are held captive in some inferior being, in an animal, in a plant, in some inanimate object, and so effectively lost to us until the day (which to many never comes) when we happen to pass by the tree or to obtain possession of the object which forms their prison. Then they start and tremble, they call us by our name, and as soon as we have recognised their voice the spell is broken. We have delivered them: they have overcome death and return to share our life' (Translated from the French by C. K. Scott Moncrieff, New York, Henry Holt and Company, 1922).

In the cloud that rises from the infusion, we have then a soul emanating from an inanimate object of the kind that the ancient Celts revered. The lost time that the writer is searching for dates to his childhood, no doubt; but he finds another that dates back to more deeply buried eras and about which he specifies the place where it is lost, trapped. The narrator's descent into the dark bowels of his personal memory coincides with the gestures and categories proper to animist cultures, foreign and deeply forgotten, long lost but now found again, civilisations and societies that were being studied during the same period by Tarde, Durkheim, Mauss and Bouglé, after Auguste Comte in France, or Sir James Frazer, with *The Golden Bough*, in Great Britain, and, in Germany, ever since the Grimm brothers and Schelling, theorists of myths and *Kultur*.

To what period does *In Search of Lost Time* go back? Stretching over a colossally longer span than the existence of an individual, this search touches eras when the worldview had nothing to do with the then contemporary prigs and salons; the great writer opens up these forgotten views for himself and brings them back before us.

Take the water-lily among the water-plants choking the course of the Vivonne. This flower attached to the bottom, propelled into the current by its stalk and periodically returning to its starting point reminds the narrator of his Aunt Léonie's 'maladies' and 'eccentricities', with her 'daily round' as 'strange' and 'ineluctable' as the 'gears' that take hold of the plant's 'green moorings', but also, but especially of the souls whose torments are 'repeated indefinitely', that Dante evokes in his *Inferno*, and those, below, about which Virgil, hastening ahead, refuses to tell him. Time lost like the dark Elysium of Antiquity.

According to Lévi-Strauss, Bergson did not hesitate to describe himself as a totemist. Proust likens himself to a Druid, first; subsequently, he tore off the Golden Bough and pictures himself in glory with the features of the priests that were said to be archaic at the time. Was he searching in this way for the time of primitivities? He found it.

As for the asparagus, whose heads were 'finely stippled in mauve and azure', they reveal themselves to be 'exquisite creatures' disguised as vegetables, endowed furthermore with the power, in their 'lyrical and coarse farces' that Shakespeare ascribes to his fairies, of transforming a 'chamber pot into a vase of perfume'. 'Iridescence', 'celestial hues', 'radiance of earliest dawn', 'blue evening shades', 'precious quality', and finally the scents of urine … they offer a glimpse of the gentleness of the soul, descended here into the kitchen, with the maid, whom Swann calls Giotto's Charity, in a basket, that of Giotto's 'Virtue at Padua'. A high and mystical soul, humble and lowly in its incarnation.

The origin of physical sciences

My own recollections, fables, and memories as told in poetry or literature, these you disdain and dismiss as arbitrarily subjective. They cannot be considered a demonstration, you say. Take a look then at objectivity, sciences and the universal. Better yet: at their very origin and their contemporary state.

No, 'naturalism' did not emerge with Galileo, neither did Galileo's work emerge from a naturalism that was then widespread or nascent. Born with his essays, mathematical physics combined, for the first time, the formal language of algebra with experimental manipulation. From this combination, as new as it was explosive, and ever since that day, so fertile that it has spawned the totality of our exact and useful knowledge, how could a radical separation arise between a uniform-mute nature and plural-talkative cultures? Who speaks there if not a mathematical language expanded in the universe and finally deciphered by us humans? Better still, sciences that, from Galilean times, were excluded from this first algebra-experiment – namely, chemistry, biochemistry, biology, and so forth – have recently been integrated into it, since a combination of codes accounts, in part, for the genesis of living beings.

What status are we to give this formal language, expressed in two dialects at least: algebra in the past, algorithms today? Couldn't we say of it that it is soft, nearly infinitesimally small, like information energy in comparison with energy on the entropic scale, which is hard and big, in contrast, like the experiment and its manipulations? Doesn't it steer the inert and the living, like the software programmes the hardware, like the soul governs the body … I mean, that it knows and can tilt its rudder at as differential an angle as Lucretius's old *clinamen*? Shouldn't we consider that – light, soft, minimal as it is, with no power other than that of signalling – it functions as a sort of spirit, like an airy breath that would animate matter, which is hard again in contrast, or even as a soul would invade bodies in order to guide them? Thus, shouldn't this invention, that Alexandre Kojève said was made possible by the dogma of Incarnation – that other soul-body combination – have launched the West toward animism instead?

What is Galileo saying when he announces that the world is written in mathematical language? That depends on the status that one gives to this language. But Galileo clearly says and we, better and more informed than he, repeat after him, that the world speaks it, writes it, copies it, and translates it. In other words, that soft mathematics codes the world, hard; it codes, like a soul, the world, like a body. Mathematics acts like the soul of the world, of things, of bodies. As information, it gives the soul a status that is precise, rigorous, transparent, luminous, ideal and, yes, eternal; its traditional status, as far as I know. Mathematics speaks the soul of a body-landscape.

To parody Spinoza, the code works like the naturing nature of natured nature.

Galileo an animist? Did the Vatican condemn him for translating into algebraic language the divine word that the Church wanted everyone – at least the vast population of illiterates – to read, with ease, in the pages of the book of the world? Had the scholarly decoder replaced the theological decipherer? No, the Galilean adventure in no way shows a 'naturalist' origin.

Galileo may not have said this, not in so many words, but Plato before him did. The demiurge in his Timaeus spoke of the world soul and fashioned its mathematical substance. But the philosopher was taking a sterile path. He believed he could deduce all things in the world as they are from the naked model of the geometry of triangles or of the rhythms of arithmetic series. He believed he could deduce the whole body from the soul alone. He believed he could see in this soul even the parts of the body, without any avatar, without any metamorphosis. But the things of the world cannot be deduced from axioms like Euclid did with his theorems.

By reversing Plato's fruitless animism, Galileo discovers the way. He starts from the body of each thing and undresses it, I dare say, to uncover, in its singularity, a given part of mathematics, a given equation, a given function. His experimentation tears open the corporeal mantle to observe, through the hole thereby created, by the particular site occupied by this body, a small mirror of the soul, that reflects, from its singular site, a partial site in the vast soul of the world.

At the time of the metamorphosis, we have the chance to see, in the passing nakedness, the soul shimmering here and there. From each experiment, a formula ensues; from each body, a part of the soul is seen. To be sure, the West has known, at least since the Greeks, that nature-body was written in the mathematical language of the soul, but only an experiment can determine what precise place of the soul, and what oblique and singular algebraic formulation are projected in what original place and what section of the body. Therein is found the true role, odd, detailed, and nearly metamorphic, of the body in all forms of animism.

For, in many longitudes, people experience the body, they think and speak of it as decisive in the continual and major flow of the soul; it alone marks discontinuities in the animated continuity – Bergson says so himself. And they wonder – and this a big question – how is it that, clothed in such a body, an individual sees the body of another? This is called perspectivism, and another great Renaissant in the classical century, Leibniz, canonised its sites. Galileo's victory consists in giving back to animism its corporeal coherence and its perspective. Plato and no doubt the Greeks missed this, overestimating as they did the powers of the soul, by which I mean of mathematics. Galileo gave it back bodies, rugged physicalities, sundry garments, a colourful multiplicity of mantels: the experiment. *The quadratic equation, this then is the angle from which solid falling bodies see, as in perspective, the whole of mathematics; thus each body carries projected fragments of the world's great mathematical soul*; a Harlequin cloak, composed of patches, each of which has a local equation written on it, like a chosen piece cut from the universal coupon of the world soul.

No, the renaissant revolution did not emerge from work or crafts, but from the multiple and discrete mathematical formatting of inorganic or animated bodies. It remains renaissant in the animist sense of the term; it remains animist, in the renaissant sense of the term. 'Naturalism' came later, much later, at least insofar as one can say that it came and conquered. It has been said that animism did not yield any power of invention, when, to the contrary, it stimulates the mind as much as analogism – both abounding sources of literary and scientific inspiration. So fertile has animism been that in it resides the origin of mechanics, mathematical physics and the experimental sciences. It consecrates the alliance of the soft, the informational, with the hard, the entropic. Of the soft, smooth and global, with the hard, local and gritty.

Contemporary sciences

At last, we have come to learn of the universal expansion of information in and through the things of the world, as through and in the gestures and deeds of humans. Be it a matter of cultures or of the object of nature, any element or aggregate *receives, emits, stores and processes information*. Without these four operations concerning information, there are no things, no world, no evolution, no life, no humans, no culture, no knowledge. In short, without these four functions, there is nothing objective, nothing cognitive, nothing collective, nothing emotive either, and perhaps nothing subjective.

On or in all the hardness of the world, expressible in strictly physical units, or even in technical, social or aesthetic terms, we can now read a code. We can decipher not only the molecules of living things, but also the crystals and particles that we once deemed inert, exactly like our own cultural archives or even like the objects that we trade in. Now all our sciences can decode the dates of their objects in the way that our histories or our archaeologies could do in the past. They can now read their memory. For all things in the world hold memories, of themselves and of others. The great book of the world opens and unfolds like a palimpsest of several thicknesses, written in several languages and often partially erased. In the deep rocks of the globe lie traces of their magnetism from the time of their cooling; radioactivity scatters and counts, almost by enumerating it, the age of the emitting body; using the brush of light, the colour of stars writes and draws their age; present here and everywhere, cosmic rays mark and trace the time of the universe. In each thing we can read, inscribed or imprinted, an anamnesis of this kind. All is memory: written, coded, imprinted, encrypted and finally readable. Hence it is received, stored, processed and finally emitted, following the four above-mentioned operations. Better yet, the things themselves know or can themselves write this code on one another, decipher it, imprint it, nearly understand it, automatically, and sometimes obey or conform to this coded command. How can we understand chemical reactions? And the fact that living cells commit suicide in response to apoptotic signalling? Information, forms of reciprocal comprehension, lurk in the world, just as similar forms move about amongst men.

We are not the only ones to read or write, the only ones to make noise with our tongues and languages, the only ones to remember, the only ones with a history, the only ones to tell stories. The Great Story of the universe includes all of our kind as partial, brief elements. All the things of the world accomplish, sometimes better than we do, the four operations, which are fundamental because they are universal, of emitting, receiving, storing and processing information. The Great Story hums with the great culture of the world. This is the final blow delivered, at the most, to the old cultural narcissism of humans or, at the least, to 'naturalist' narcissism.

Exceptional, nonetheless, we know how to build machines that, like the things of the world, receive, emit, store and process information and that, for these four reasons, can be called universal. Yes, we make machines to mimic all things, natural and cultural alike. We can no longer comprehend the subject of comprehension itself; we will no longer be able to know the cognitive itself without trying to comprehend how we managed to gain a handle on that mimicking.

Would it be a mark of reprehensible daring to call the soul of the world this information, present everywhere, perhaps even at the origin of all, stored in all places, processed by all bodies, emitted and received everywhere and always, like background noise, and circulating in space-time in such a way that all bodies, including ours, including our ways of comprehending, receive a part of it and emit another? Without this informational soul, truly unitary though divisible into a thick fog of bits or pixels, there are no differentiated bodies, no landscaped universe, no real singularities, no world body, no language, no culture, no knowledge. Knowledge and existence flow from a single source.

All is information. All is code. All is number: here we are Pythagoreans again. Does an animism accompany contemporary knowledge? Not really ‘it from bit’, an expression that signifies an origin, but, better still, ‘it with bits’, which describes an immanentism.

Relations and religions

If I sometimes dream that music expresses the breeze with wordless sounds of the soul of the world, I want to end, by caution of reason, with religions.

We've all observed an interesting shift, over a few generations, in the interpretation of the pagan gods of our antiquity. In the past, our masters saw them as symbols of fertility, images of harvests and vineyards ... of plant life. As much peasants, I mean pagans, as the Ancients themselves, those scientists continued to speak of the power of mute life in plants and animals. Animists? Similarly, when the French Revolution sought to replace the Gregorian calendar, celebrating the life of Jesus Christ and thick with saints, they listed harvests, vintages, flowers, mists, winds and meadows. It was as if Bergson's *élan vital* was already circulating through the course of the rural year.

The same gods of the same mythology, we see them today as scapegoats of our enterprises of violence. As much peasants as they were, our ancestors called the gods of paganism of the Ancients peasants. Living as we do now in cities, having abandoned, like most of our contemporaries, frosts and fruits, we can no longer speak of these gods save in terms of politics or social science. What hatreds, the ones with and against the others, adhere to us as a result? In the past we saw the old Pantheon as a summary of natural sciences or rural practices; now we see it only as a compendium of human sciences.

Are they the same gods? How is it, good god, that Jupiter (*Ju-Piter*, meaning Day-Father) associates, in his very name and in his functions, the serene clarity of the day with the love or hatred of the Father? What is the meaning of the comma, added or omitted, between 'Our Father' and 'Who art in heaven'? How is it that we think, love, know, act ... in short, that we live a culture under the hard light of nature, this at the same time and in a single *élan*? What is the meaning of this deep-seated relationship that the word religion modulates and repeats? What is the meaning of this global connection that can also be called analogy?

I, analogist monad

'My name is Legion'
Mark 5:9; Luke 8:30

Another autobiography

Even though totemism and its classifications seem quite alien to me, even though I had to endure the exclusivity of naturalism in the institutions where I taught, I consider that I belong to an animist family. Heir to a farming and sailing people, familiar with high seas and high mountains, this worldview enchants me. The cows that my brother and I tended all had names and characteristic personalities. Some, the dominant ones, were the first to return to the barn, while others, more submissive, lagged behind; we didn't milk the brave and fat cow the same way as the one that was thin, nervous and jealous. It was the same with the horses, pigs and roosters. When we spoke of the sea, whose fury assaulted the boat and whose lulls turned it into paradise, we called it a cruel mistress or a tender-hearted lover. How do we caress the rock, when the grip surges over the smooth, if not as a surprising mistress? I end here the confession of my private temptations.

For, with blind certainty, all my life I've built a philosophy that would put me in the tribe of analogists. Formerly at ease in the Greek deployment of the multiplicities of the world related to Plato's ideas or to Plotinus's hypostases; or running, moved, through the interlacing of the moved and moving, causing and caused things of the world, in the Stoics; even more comfortable in Leibniz's pluralism, so illuminating for contemporary knowledge, I haunt the latter, that I see more and more stripped of naturalism due to the results obtained by algorithmic thinking and technologies; yes, I inhabit analogism like a paradise that fills me with joy. Unequivocally, all the books I have written unite me with this team.

Definitions

For these tribes, undefined aggregates of disparates exist, corporeal or incorporeal. Surviving, acting and thinking amid such confusion involves the exhausting obligation of working relentlessly at composition, of seeking thousands of relationships capable of bridging these differences. In this chapter, analogy formally designates the aggregate of these possible connections.

The mixed, striped, flecked, many-hued, many-coloured, multi-patterned, motley kaleidoscope of these disparates is scattered everywhere, in the objective world as in the collective and cognitive world, the welling up of countless aggregates whose elements are differentiated down to the tiniest detail. I have never stopped striving to bridge the evident span produced by a connected or torn network, in any case overloaded with communications, interferences, translations, broad or strangled passageways, bridges and prepositions. Several figures embody these mediations in traversing several of these interlacings: Hermes, god of merchants, thieves and translators; angels and demons; parasites and symbionts; a whole slew of messengers … Jesus Christ himself, the mediator *par excellence* … under the historical patronage of Leibniz, the first philosopher of communication, and amid the noise of our contemporaries, exchanging their messages today on the Web. Our new technologies adapt beautifully to that knowledge and to that world.

Thus constellated with singularities, this ever-changing fabric inspires me and resembles reality as it is, or at least as I see it and think of it, textured, but also as I live it, laugh it, cry it and hope it. I swim with joy in an ocean of disparates, strewn with pathways, here and there. In this picture that I have been trying to paint for five decades, I recognise the sumptuous unfolding of the world and I recognise myself, for, if and when I think, I connect the throng or the chaos of these strong, streaming differentiations by relations or by bridges of all kinds, including with others. I lose myself in this festivity, panting for breath and never managing to embrace a profusion from which a flow is always escaping. I seek a key and find only thousands. But if I found only one, I'd be suspicious of this burglar's trip wire.

Here is my name and my signature: I am called Nobody, Passepartout, Pantope, the one who hastens or who wanders in all places; better still, Legion, as numerous and differentiated as any other person and, around me, as all things of the world or, in me, all thoughts. '*Mon âme aux mille voix, que le Dieu que j'adore / Mit au centre de tout comme un écho sonore*' ('My soul with a thousand voices, that the God I love / Put in the centre of all like a resounding echo'). Vertigos in this vortex. *Cogito*, Descartes said; through me pass a multiplicity of thoughts, replied Leibniz, more expert in etymology. Indeed, what does *cogitation* mean, if not *co-agitation*, the vertiginous disorder of a herd of thousands of sheep that one shepherd alone cannot drive or lead, *agere*? This Latin verb means to drive animals, whose agitation comes from being together with many others, which then become hard to manage. Yes, all my life, thought, with its chaotic, streaming, luminous composite, background noise, has never stopped making my head spin. It has me reeling, stumbling, trembling, it bowls me over, dizzy and dazzled. Rivers and turbulence, joy.

Disparate aggregates

Our literature is teeming with these thousands of aimless disparate aggregates: the marquetry of lists in Rabelais; the mosaic of *Essays* in Montaigne; the discrete jewels in La Fontaine's *Fables*; contingent sideroads down which Jacques the Fatalist dashes; the *Encylopédie* with no other order than the alphabet for the century of the Enlightenment; I will soon revisit Flaubert's displays, from *The Temptation of Saint Anthony* to the bedroom-cum-museum of Félicité, Simple Soul, from the altar where the parrot is perched to Bouvard and Pécuchet's disorderly knowledge, to the copies of their foolishness – did Flaubert invent there the hypertext?; the labyrinth in which the Chants de Maldoror lose their way; the refuse fields and the inextricable barbed wire in Tournier; *Life: A User's Manual* ... All disparates awaiting relations.

Disparates in literature enchant me, as do the painted hell or feasts, in Breughel's or Bosch's Flanders, in Matisse's collages, Stravinsky's music and more. The analogist heroine, as anyone can see, is Ariadne, the image of a woman giving a stupid, brawny, lost male a clue so he can find his way through the labyrinth prior to action, to the world and to thought ... ; a male so detestable that, hurrying to resume his journey through the disparate and to lose his way again, he abandons on the shore his beatific and life-saving companion.

The optimist composer: Leibniz

My model of the analogist philosopher, and no doubt the precise precursor of contemporary inventors, wrote *Monadology* to say expressly that nothing but singularities existed, all different, and all windowless and doorless, stripped of any connection between them. Likewise, for him, the mind of God contains an infinity of possible disparates and the real world, indiscernible things *ad infinitum*. Leibniz spent most of his life defying the two labyrinths of infinity and freedom, bridging all possible disparates by harmonic connections that he summarises and unites at the vanishing point of divine transcendence. He ended it by inventing a last connection, the substantial bond, while never ceasing to list programmes, to project alphabets, dictionaries, letting himself thereby be overcome by the proliferation of all things, beyond any *Mathesis universalis*. Infinite pluralism connected by a universal harmony.

At the beginning of his *On the Combinatorial Art*, where, at a young age, he began to examine the most formal connections, Leibniz draws the hot-cold, dry-wet square as taught by the Rosicrucians; we know of no Mayan from Yucatan, no Dogon from Mali who does not classify disparates according to these opposites. He was eighteen and, already, he was constructing an analogic combinatorial concept to turn green with envy a Tzotzil, a Bambara, or a biochemist confronted today with the combinatory explosion in living systems.

Immersed in the disparate and finding no general connection save in God, he could never compose a book except on the canvas of another, nor write a text than the world itself in recounting its creation by God, the sole calculator and arbiter among the infinity of possible worlds and the sole federator of messages in languages. A collection of boxes remains in the cellars of Hanover where a thousand and one details of Leibnizianism sleep still, unpublished, unrelated. Pessimism at what remains to be examined or optimism at the best that has already been filtered out?

I live, dream and think in the family of these analogists, thinkers and artists as alien to naturalism as the scholars in China or the pre-Columbian Nahuas. Did I ever feel happier than in the environs of Alice Springs where, racing across the desert in the Australian outback in the company of Aborigenes, I should have met, black and wildly painted, Flaubert and Tournier, Lautréamont and Rabelais, Aristotle and Leibniz, asking themselves how to cover with connections these kaleidoscopes, as abandoned to chaos as the world and self-awareness, and what interlacings to compose from these disparates? This is the true project of their works, it is surely the horizon of mine, so close to the Dreaming of those natives. So close, finally, to the hypertexts exhibited everywhere on the web of our recent technologies. The contemporary intersects the wild, our cousin.

Seeking to consider, from these mingled bodies, an immediate example, my *Five Senses* passed through forests where 'perfumes, sounds, and colours correspond', 'Like prolonged echoes mingling in the distance /In a deep and tenebrous unity /Vast as the dark of night and as the light of day'. 'There are perfumes as cool as the flesh of children /Sweet as oboes, green as meadows'.

Do these rhythms repeat analogism's worldview, and mine too, or do they recite, quickly, Charles Baudelaire's most famous verses, whose sonnet intersects in the forest of *Correspondences* and to draw its plan, the perfect temple of this rite, the temple whose pillars simulate trees? Spirit and meaning are transported there into the interlacing of relations that unite thousands of disparate sensations. At least the poet tries to sense an order there, like a composition, through symbols and words.

More concretely, in the same book, I'd defended *confusion*, so unfairly condemned by analytic and separatist thinking. Why disdain a mingling that can lead to excellence and where it is less a matter of correspondence than of the confluence – the noble version of the ignoble confusion – of the juices of many different grapes from different vine stocks flowing together to compose a rare wine? What river would deprive itself of affluents? What effective remedy, of components? What blood, even blood that a racist hymn deems impure, does not descend from a mix? The adverb concretely expresses, in its own way, this same confluence, this same impurity, this same mix, not for fluids but, more subtly, for solids, which accrete. Astronomers say that the Earth itself was formed, concretely, from such an accretion. Whoever seeks the concrete will find the confused.

The analogist traces relations in 'the dark of night and the light of day,' separated; he seeks 'a deep and tenebrous unity' precisely amidst 'confused words': the one who forms this bouquet for *Les Fleurs du mal* (1857), let us call him the composer.

Flaubert, the pessimistic composer

In that same period, Gustave Flaubert spent twenty-five years writing *The Temptation of Saint Anthony* (1874), inspired by Breughel's painting of the same name and which associated, once again, disparate discontinuities to depict the manifold hell of desire. What a bizarre literary form the *Temptation* is! Aesthetic but also cognitive, epistemic, technical, real, global and more. A muddle, a jumble, a museum, a bazaar? More like Wikipedia! Everything is found there, like, for Leibniz, in the mind of God; like in Félicité's room with its jumble of souvenirs of her life piled up in disorder; like on the altar of Corpus Christi where her stuffed parrot is perched alongside flowers and a monstrance; like in the woods in *Julian* where the corpses of hunted animals are heaped up; like at the feast of Hérodias or of *Salammbô*; like in *Bouvard and Pécuchet* for the sciences ... like on the Web ... like in the world.

You can find everything in the world, you can find everything on the Web, you can find everything in Leibniz, you can find everything in Flaubert, you can find everything at the *Bonheur des Dames*, where the owner, no doubt based on Boucicaut, overturns all categories one morning, in a flash of inspiration, and thereby makes his fortune. What name would there be for a philosophy in which you cannot find everything? Not only do you find everything and everybody in every place but also the question of relationships, in an open-ended, absent and problematical way. You can find all of these relationships in the list of prepositions, this dazzling treasure that opens, in a virtual way, onto a nearly complete set of connections; in this list, philosophy resides. This is also the secret of *The Temptation of Saint Anthony*: to open up and deploy the totality of religions, that is to say of the channels of connection (*re-ligare*, re-connect). This is the secret of *Bouvard and Pécuchet*: to open up the disparate totality of knowledge, of that upon which the totality of relations (*re-ligere*) that can compose it can be deployed or not; whoever fails at this enterprise remains in the pure disparate disorder of facts; as such, he becomes bovine – Bouvard, Bovary – or returns to the herd, *pecus* – Pécuchet. Bull-headed foolishness.

As intelligently sharp as his perception was, and as truly perspicacious and even realistic as his intuition of the disorderly elements of the world, of religion, of knowledge and of humans became, nonetheless Flaubert seems, at first glance, to see nothing in the disparate but a consistent failure of relations. To be sure, he composes madly, to be sure, he composes marvellously, but he despairs of the success of a single connection. His savants distribute and enlist knowledge without any connection, which makes them foolish ... Homais, Bouvard, Pécuchet; they *bovaryse* his lovers, with loveless relations; Saint Anthony loses himself in the open-ended array of heretical choices; we laugh, with bitterness, at the accepted ideas that circulate; bovine stupidity prevails over a composite with no possible composition … Flaubert lacks Ariadne: he's left dazzled by a specific vertigo, reduced to an analogism without analogy. His pessimism is not subjective in the least; on the contrary, his despair is based on a deep-seated reason, a sentiment that Leibniz also complained about sometimes, calling it distraction. This word expresses, better than vertigo or turbulence, the pathology that characterises our analogist tribe: everything distracts us, attracts our interested attention elsewhere and otherwise. Although Flaubert glimpses, with precision and without a doubt, the incomparable wealth of disparate sets and in this, powerfully, our knowledge, our techniques and our contemporary world, he does not seem to want to believe in the possibility of a desmology, in a general theory of the bonds that would unify them. Would nothing exist other than the unbound, the *decomposed* – 'And others, corrupt, rich and triumphant / With power to expand into infinity' … Unlike *Correspondences*, I cannot draw or paint a network, Flaubert seems to say, in opposition to Leibniz, regarded as an optimistic philosopher, who owes this trait, incidentally a bit foolish, to the fact that he calculates and draws networks of relations. There is nothing without a reason, he says: this saves him from sinking into the disparate. Leibniz, Ariadne, saved; Theseus, Flaubert, lost.

Yet, and this is the horizon of the glimpsed possible analogy, Madame Bovary dreams of amorous relations,

Bouvard and Pécuchet chase after related knowledge, Saint Anthony prays to the Transcendent …

Where there are relations, there's reason. *If the real is* rational, *relations* (ratios) *saturate, subtend, solidify it like a crystal. But all is not calculable; there is contingency. If the real is* relational, related, religious, *there can be connections* (re-ligare) *of all orders through the real.* Broader, vaguer, less dominated, even indefinite, the second hypothesis includes the first, narrower, more defined, rigorous, effective, controlled.

Our world: databases

In the gritty world of disparate objects, in human societies where individuals-monads, windowless and doorless, do not listen, speak, or understand, how could we keep from trying to trace connections, and even pondering the generality of them? How could we keep from being fascinated by communication, relentlessly inventing passageways, dreaming of a desmology, of a general philosophy of connection, inflected by prepositions? Whoever thinks, writes, lives, soon becomes a *composer*. Optimistic: the composition prevails over the disparate; pessimistic: the latter brims over the former. This composer will never cease, therefore, from forging, so as to assume correspondences and personages: Hermes, the parasite, the symbiote, Pantope, angels ...; iron or concrete tools: bridges ...; or formal tokens of sorts, small tools capable of sculpting language: those prepositions again.

Informatics organises the best tool of the composer. The global Web hosts, gathers, assembles and covers disparate sets. Complainers grumble to see this composite, this disparate, this conceptless and shameless mess. They should reread Rabelais, Leibniz or Flaubert, or slowly turn over by hand the pages of encyclopaedias and dictionaries. These old collections, all disparate, have no other order than alphabetical, whereas, equipped with means of navigation launched at the speed of light – the apex of analogy – we lose our way less in this new sea than we did in libraries, less copious though they were. Better yet, on this atomised ocean of bits and pixels, every individual-monad can express himself, post his blog, display his face, develop his knowledge, surf together with other monads-individuals. Better still, extending the metaphor of light as illustrating knowledge, here its speed supplants its clarity. We used to need diagrams and categories, concepts to master the number and the different; we are no longer afraid of confronting, in real time, the throng of singularities without connections. The speed of light federates.

We now live among the aggregates, foreseen and prepared by Rabelais, Leibniz, Diderot and Flaubert, in a world as undefined as it is splintered, plunged in a sea, an ocean, a tsunami of data, which we can hardly master and can only begin to do so with the support of computer software. The huge quantity of these databanks exceeds, and by far, our processing abilities. We navigate across these open seas by means of a tool that can be defined as a universal mime of every object in the world, as a network of relations, perhaps also as a mime of our brain. To the multiplied sea of disparate things corresponds a tight interlacing of human, formal and technical relations, constantly multiplying, with means chasing after data that remains to be processed, without, for the moment, being able to catch up with it.

This continual struggle between a vertiginous ocean and the networks of relations that are continually multiplying their connections rigorously defines analogism, a word that perfectly summarises and depicts our objective world, our cognitive works, our subjective dreams as well as the collectives that are emerging today and that will determine the politics of tomorrow. In philosophy, literature and the arts, this world, our world, has been long in the making.

What science made it possible?

Origins of mathematical sciences

Let's start over again; let's leave behind confessions, thoughts or stories, and get back on the road of demonstration where we learn a thing or two about the origins of geometry.

Constructing or imagining the abstraction of a sky of pure ideas does not suffice for mathematics to emerge and indefinitely pursue the dynamics of its development. Connections must be established that are capable of relating the different elements of disparate multiplicities, ideal or real. For the Greeks of this miraculous moment, the *logos* exceeds, and by far, the paleoanthropological use and operation of language or speech, to designate, in a new way, proportion, the fraction *a/b* and, very soon, reason, in the sense of the relationship between two elements or diverse marks *a* and *b*. Indeed, the said *logos*, the proportion, rigorously defines the first reason-relation that connects *a* and *b* together. As a result, this *logos* launches, as a starting point, a vast series, that of relations or connections, yes, reasons that, in mathematics, will signify an ever-renewed variety of equivalences: equality, parallelism, equation, parity, homothety, overlapping, similitude, invariance, isomorphy, homeomorphy, modulo equivalence, *p*-adic numbers ... This series never ends.

Given that the world and the mind are evidently brimming over with disparates, what a novelty, what a discovery, both prime and decisive, to find the felicitous language that can establish formal relations between these components. Thus languages, to begin with, helped us. *Thus mathematics, a universal and global language, saved us.* Universal because it is formal and sayable by all, regardless of cultural differences, but also global because it is strewn with irrationals, transcendentals, imaginaries, undecidables, as the universe is strewn with dark matter, the counting of prime numbers or the history of unforeseen events. Mathematics launches a pure, transparent and supple analogist language for an analogist world, strewn with singularities as it is. Thence we understand the correspondence between it and the world, which enables our comprehension of the world, a correspondence that Kant and Einstein deemed miraculous.

From the outset, these relations teemed in this language: the second, after the *logos*, called *analogon*, expresses the equality of two proportions, $a/b = c/d$. This elementary equation quickly become the centrepiece of all demonstrations, in pure pre-Euclidian geometry, in the *Elements* themselves and for a long time thereafter. Was nascent mathematics rigorously sanctifying in this way the analogist worldview? Or did this view help it discover *logos*, proportion, and *analogon*, concepts to which mathematics owes its birth in part, to be sure, but also its inexhaustible dynamism, its history even, since the path thus begun is continually encountering differentiated elements to the point of contradiction that a new effort of relating seeks to bridge?

An example, from the start: the scandal of irrationals, that will launch Platonism, designates, conversely, the overstepping of the *logos* and even of the analogy, by a difference, literally infinite, of certain elements that neither one nor the other can calculate or dominate. The first demonstration in due form, the one that leads to an absurdity, discovers the irrationality of the diagonal of a square with side 1: as if reason or proportion, full of holes, was leaking an infinite series of lawless numbers. Already, the disparate brims over the relation. A choice had to be made between a calculation, *logos*, proportion or reason, that fails, and that Plato will leave, not without a degree of contempt, to the little slave in *Meno*, and a rigorous demonstration that Socrates and the entire history to come of mathematics will adopt.

As a result, rigorous reason prevails over calculation or, more precisely, the declarative prevails over the algorithmic and the die is cast for two millennia or nearly. Theodorus, Theaetetus and Plato himself come to the rescue of analogy, whose triumph, again, over difference marks another elementary stage in the tension between the disparate and reason or relation that punctuates, like a dynamism between an obstacle and a will, the history of this science, up to and including structuralism.

Perennial, in effect, in the history of mathematics, this rational and relational celebration is a reminder that the structuralism defined by anthropologists, several decades ago in Paris, intersected the structuralism of Bourbaki, the formalist algebraist and topologist, and even of Dumézil, the historian of religions. By playing with analogy, and in its widest range and its powerful formalism, it was a matter, in all cases, of comparing sets, provided with operations, often drawn from areas as different as geometry and number theory for Bourbaki, and India and Rome for Dumézil, to bring out their common operational functioning. Whereas the former was linked to totemism, the kind that Lévi-Strauss analysed and that we encountered in the first chapter of this book, the latter had a deep-seated relationship with that analogism. Working on maximally differentiated, complex and numerous multiplicities, it accomplished miracles when it came to establishing relationships between things that at first, second, or umpteenth glance had none. A case in point: the structure of order makes it possible to relate upstream and downstream, the irreversibility of a mixture or of a disorder, that of passing time, engenderment and kinship, royal power and any hierarchy … a unique order in the diverse that is demonstrated in the dialogue opposing predator and prey in *The Wolf and the Lamb*. Varied in multiple ways, the key and repeated operation of mathematics, I reiterate, consists in finding homotheties, equalities, isomorphs ... bridging the greatest known differences. In algebra or in topology, the structures straddled the widest known differences. It was the greatest effort of this time in the act of understanding. As usual, mathematics paved the way. In this, it remained faithful to its origin and to the dynamism of its development.

As we know, Kant and Einstein wondered by what mystery mathematics succeeds so well in understanding the world. Here is the clear answer to this question: all you have to do is define this exquisite discipline as the highest, as the most rigorous language, as the best equipped to state and diversify any analogic relation, in short an organon of ways of expressing relations, ratios, equations, applications, equalities, reciprocities, endomorphs, equivalences, invariances ... in constant progression toward a completeness aspiring to cover multiplicities of growing differentiation, finding their best expression in – literally fundamental – set theory. Mathematics never stops bridging the differences between these disparate collections, outlining a universal atlas of ways; these ways are called methods in Greek; mathematics writes thousands of discourses of as many methods. If understanding means establishing relationships then the world, flowing with sets of highly differentiated singularities, encounters there one of the extremely rare, and perhaps the only, language that manages to bridge its own differences – as well as those of the outside – in a rigorous and ever renewed way. Mathematics fits into the category of analogism, not only since its origin, not only throughout its history, not only today, but almost in its very definition. Conversely, analogism is a mathematism.

Newton worked a similar miracle in tracing a simple path between solids falling and the planetary orbits. Who would have believed – and the Académie de Paris did not – in such an effortless and universal trajectory? Bohr himself compared these orbits with the circulations of particles around the nucleus of atoms. Even though this model partially failed, analogism had nonetheless inspired its author. Let us generalise. Once the encyclopaedia, without order, opens its integral, spatial and circular horizon to a story of the Universe, creating a chain from the big bang, already dated, to the whole series of datings that contemporary knowledge has observed, then a landscape of unsuspected variety unfolds before our eyes, connected by a grandiose scale of time. Our sciences establish in this way, no doubt, across innumerably disparate multiplicities, the most general and longest of maximally continuous connections, albeit broken into unforeseen and contingent bifurcations. Chaos theory made it possible to establish this powerful and flexible, interminable chronological bond.

Now holding in its hands all the sciences and the world, the Great Story recounts, in the finest detail and the boldest summing up, the most complete expression of analogism.

Yet another origin? The gradual discontinuity of the elements that compose existing things, the exchanges of these parts between the external and the internal, as well as between two interiorities, or yet again between two separate things, *partes extra partes*, show that change takes place either by metamorphosis – and in this case we have evolutionism, with its operations of mutation and selection that produce species, following a somewhat animist or vitalist *élan vital* – or by possession – and here we have exchanges of parts which I will discuss shortly, but also equations of sorts that balance the reactions between composed, decomposed, then reshaped bodies, and finally recomposed element by element. To the origins of geometry, can we associate – oh wonder! – those of chemistry? Newton's exploit, I'm not forgetting him, came from a head and hands that practiced alchemy, the mad analogism which preceded that of the rationally more sensible chemistry.

Just as metamorphosis characterises animism, so possession distinguishes analogism. Parts that compose the self detach from it and wander here and there through the vast world, whose things are also composed of moving and traveling parts, capable of settling, here and there, in other people or things, including in the self. Before arriving at so-called demonic possession, let us dwell again on these compositions and decompositions.

The universal differentiation that makes everything that exists a singularity that resembles none other must be explained. A set of first pieces enables, through thousands of combinations, the production, in throngs, of these diverse varieties. Let us set aside, for the moment, the microcosm of the body, which, due to the original composition of elements, coming from everywhere, that it unites and densifies, is given the status of reduced model of the global macrocosm. Let us focus, instead, on the simple dynamics of the decomposition into traveling elements, and the recomposition elsewhere – and on another objective – of the same or other elements, combined in the same or in other ways. This is the programme of *On the Combinatorial Art*, the first act of Leibnizian analogism; but the method, too, of all chemistry, starting from simple bodies and recombining them as many times as the combinatory explosion opens it, in the indefinite.

And, quite precisely, the same is true of people, composed in this way of multiple parts. Here I am constructed from these disparate elements, from which my person creates, so to speak, a synthesis, but none of the elements of which are specifically attached to me. Each of them can enter or leave and enter at leisure another person, whose self it will then contribute to constructing. The metamorphosis transforms Proteus into a lion, panther, boar or snake, or even a linden tree, water or wind; possession deconstructs a person and reconstructs the individual from other elements that may come from or belong to another or to others.

It puts one in mind of a chemical reaction. And, also, of the way the cards are shuffled when the parental genes mix during sexual reproduction! We have here what is clearly a schema of origin, not of knowledge but of some living things. We are all mixes, to be sure; are we all possessed?

Last autobiography: the possessed of Gerasa

Refrain: just as metamorphosis characterises animism, so possession distinguishes analogism. The attention that philosophy compelled me, at times, to focus on myself often led to these two avatars. Young, I became a fish. I now confess the extent to which attentive tension made me enter, partially often and sometimes totally, a particular person, idea or thing. Jacques Monod complained to me that he had a backache, so possessed had he been by the DNA or RNA ribbons twisting, on their model, his spinal cord, fixated on his studies. To find myself alienated in this way by what I was obsessively thinking about was something I've experienced many a time. Without this, could one invent? *I think, therefore I am other.* Concentrated, focused, centred around and on this other, to the point that it penetrates one's body. Precisely alienated. Let's face it! We may very well create only what comes out of ourselves; but if it comes out, then it must have gone in. This is how my soul, among all those that think, can speak with many voices.

Common and dark, this obsession reaches its height when passion makes a particular woman penetrate the body to the point of alienation; I've got you under my skin! Mistress possessor, she owns the person who thereby finds himself torpedoed by a kind of narcissist and narcotic demon. Invaded. Occupied. Held. Drinking the potion down to its very dregs. The elixir enters the thorax, drop by drop; the woman enters, part by part.

Jesus found me not far from Gerasa. Naked, wandering, unstable, having broken free of every chain, haunting the tombs cut in the rock, crying out, begging God to never drive out of me this manifold woman as intelligently differentiated as an occupation army, fulfilling all functions. I love you, therefore I am your host; I beg you, live in me, eat me, I give you my self to devour, warm yourself at my basic metabolism. Did I want it. Did she want it? What does it matter? She possessed me. *Invita invitum immisit.*

Jesus found me not far from Gerasa. Naked, wandering, unsteady, having broken free of every chain, haunting the tombs cut in the rock, crying out, begging God to never drive out of me all these men. Chinese, pre-Columbian Nahuas, Tzotzil of Mayan language, Chortis of Guatemala, Dogons and Bambaras of the Voltaic-Mande area, in West Africa, all of them analogists like me, occupying my soul with thousands of voices, singing, like them, the sumptuous world of the indiscernible and the multiple relations covered by an infinitely criss-crossing interlacing. I think therefore I am their thoughts. I love them, they are my hosts; they haunt me, devour me, warm themselves at my skin. Did I want it? Did they want it? What does it matter? They possess me. *Inviti invitum immiserunt.*

Circe the magician metamorphosed the companions of Ulysses, he too known by the name Nobody and Passepartout. But him, Ulysses, the sorcerer could not penetrate; him, her potion could not disturb. As for the members of his crew, she changed them into swine. Homer does not say how they lived and if they died in these new clothes. Metamorphosis of sailors, one by one; possession of a person by multiplicities. The three synoptic Gospels say that the demons, when they went out of the poor naked demoniac, entered the bodies of a hundred pigs, rushed down a steep slope and drowned in the sea or in the lake. Panurge's sheep, devils of imitation, demons of death. In committing suicide, does the possessed believe, that just as vermin and lice disappear in the shower, that he can thus get rid of his occupants, the innumerable throng, or of his guest multiplied by a mortal imitation?

A large herd was grazing on the mountain, Saint Luke says. The experience of possession elicits the feeling of having this multiplicity, this herd, this countless agitated mass inside oneself, clambering in a hellish racket … 'essaim des Djinns qui passe / Et tourbillonne en sifflant' ('swarm of Jinns passing through / Whirling and whistling') … Jesus asks him, 'What is your name?' 'I am Legion,' the poor man replied, infested by a regiment of demons … 'Hideuse armée / De vampires et de dragons!' ('Hideous army / of vampires and dragons')

Outside, the infinite plurality of things, its kaleidoscope, and the intersecting network of their relations, project their clamorous chaos, disordered-ordered, into the innermost being of the subject, in the throes, as much as the world, of the deafening tohu-bohu of buzzings and background noise.

A multitude of thoughts agitate in me, says Leibniz. Does Descartes see that his *cogito* hides an old *co-agito* whose first meaning designates the chaotic movement of a huge herd of sheep? My thoughts, my sluts, says Denis Diderot, as he admires their passage, in procession, at the Palais Royal; I am Legion, says the possessed of Gerasa, a huge mass of pigs agitate, cogitate inside me. Again: 'My soul with a thousand voices, that the God I love / Put in the centre of all like a resounding echo.'

Thus total parts of her and of them escape her and them and enter into me; thus pieces of me come out, galloping herd. I am Legion, Harlequin in cut-up rags, dismembered body, nearly quartered, ripped to shreds like Orpheus by frenzied Thracian women, in danger of falling from on high, down my steep slope into the lake of my scattered tears or tumbling down the descent into hell.

Orpheus's head, it is said, continued for a long time to sing as it floated down the current, the bed of a slow river. Ever since these animals plunged all together into the sea, the sea becomes like the stem or the composite metaphysics that I dream of; divine and smiling, this sea mingles, this I live, I see, at least I know, all possible thoughts; its tidal murmur speaks like me, thinks and sings in many voices.

Nuptials of nature and culture

Philippe Descola terms naturalism the common worldview in the West, for which original human consciousness and intimacy, as well as the diverse cultures of the world, are separated from things and bodies, all uniformly composed of atoms. Active and endowed with interiority, personal or collective humans – subjects – perceive, observe, feel, think, know and intentionally transform objects, which are exterior and passive.

This huge divorce between us, different in feelings, languages, rites and institutions, depending on the civilisation, and these things, all smooth and similar because they are composed of the same ingredients is what would characterise the West. Nature, on one side; cultures, on the other. The other three ways of seeing, visited earlier, ignore this division, from which we have gained what we call objectivity.

Subject, here; objects, opposite. But what do these words mean?

Object, thing, reality

The scholastic university of our Middle Ages, and Oresme no doubt, invented this first separation, subject-object, under the influence, they say, of the Judeo-Christian religion. Here are two words of Latin origin built on a verb: *jacere*, to throw; *ob-ji(a) cere,* to throw before; *sub-ji(a)cere*, to throw under. The object designates what is found thrown before the subject who lies underneath.

The preposition *ob* sets up an op-position: against, opposite … Impartial ob-servation, perhaps, but also ob-struction, ob-stacle, ob-jection, even ob-session. This prefix of separation can thus yield meanings contrary to what we believe characterises objectivity. Example: in defining the grammatical *object*, we replace the old Latin *accusative*, whose name – the cause! – evokes a confrontation and smacks of the prosecutor in the court of law: 'Objection!' Cries the public accuser, the very same one that is called Satan in Hebrew. Here is a passionate battle, a subjective intention that greatly disturbs the purported impartial impersonality of the thing as such.

And what can be said of objects *themselves*? These things, *choses* say the French, that we think of and see as objective, repeat the *causes* – it's the same word – the accusations, again, before the tribunal sitting in judgment. Better yet: the *res*, the thing that realism brandishes before it, as a guarantee of objectivity, firstly means a judged matter: the cause of a trial, the lawsuit, the object of litigation. In sum, the very words of objectivity resonate with thousands of arguments heard in courts of justice, penal and civil.

Personal intentions, subjective passions, even aggressiveness, also fill the meaning of the word thus thrown before – *ob-jectus* – like a view, a perspective related therefore to a point of view, to begin with, then the meaning of the love flame '*volage adorateur de mille objets divers*' ('*fickle lover of a thousand different objects*') says Racine of Theseus, or '*l'unique object de mon ressentiment*' ('*sole object of my resentment*') Camille protests against the Eternal City in *Horace*. Aesthetics, now: Balzac was the first to speak of the *objet d'art*.

It was as if language, since the Middle Ages, had been warning our sociologists of science whose analyses inflate the objectivity of individual, collective and political subjectivities; this, at least, has been clearly expressed by the terms themselves for more than a millennium, and has been lingering in their meanings ever since. In saying *object, thing, real*, three words of juridical origin, we think our language is stepping back in cold and lucid analyses, when in fact it is haunting passions and disputes. The 'naturalist' divorce breaks down.

In citing law as it does, could it be that this divorce simply comes from the fact that Barbarians, animals, material things and nature itself, incapable of becoming legal subjects, fall into the category of objects? In the final analysis, what tribunal dictates our objects of study? What *critique* makes this determination? Conversely, wouldn't naturalism die from a Natural Contract? It renders this pact unthinkable.

And so we pretend that real things or objects remain insensitive and deaf to other uses of these terms of objectivity. To be sure, we try to reduce these harmonics; and often, we succeed; sometimes we even manage, in speaking the language of applied mathematics, to put the world and things at a distance from us, as individuals or collectivities. A worthy and rare purging. The very realism that I readily profess projects those things and that world to an asymptotic limit, if it exists, where we hope to reach that realism, by a heroic, historic, infinite effort, by a continual smoothing over of these contradictory meanings. The real world seems to us to appear on the horizon of that undertaking. We practice it, indicate it, teach it, seek to transmit it. But would we survive in a world where there would be nothing but these objects?

Here are some concrete examples. Western naturalism is said to have descended from a number of techniques, from windmills, watermills, steam mills, in short, from mechanical models, from machines. Here, then, is one: the watch. It's a constructed object, perfected by Huyghens, who added an escapement to the mechanism, and who would be, precisely, nearly the first to bring objectivity into the most intimate subjectivity, into the ever so fluctuating consciousness of time, and even into the organisation of a number of social practices. Thanks to him, we would invent timetables. The young Descartes, during the same period, celebrated such automata as the geared machines that decorated public gardens at the time. Once its springs are wound up, the clock works by itself; it is self-propelled. Admirable piece of work!

Animals function this way, wound up by God, says Descartes. Now the surrounding world, the sun and the planets, turn similarly, though we can't see their motor. Automata, animals, function like machines; likewise, the world runs and spins like a watch. At the sight of these fabrications, how can we avoid the model of the beast-machine or of the world-clock? The mechanism projects onto nature and life the schema of automata. Conversely, machines imitate the movements of the heavens. The world expands these fabrications to its dimensions by figures and movements. Naturalism expresses, at one go, the built and the given.

What I've called 'the format' appears. The Venitian *quattrocento* invented several sorts: perspective and the revival of conic sections (not, as is often said, invented by painters, but rediscovered through Arabic translation of the treatise by Apollonius) for space, the printing press in language, currency in trade, accounting for commerce, and so on. Motion transmission mechanisms and the emerging science of statics or kinematics form only a part of this formatting that gives Europe the tools of intervention – the press, the clock, tables, checks, balance sheets, sundry units of measurement, etc. – of unparalleled efficiency. The homogeneity of objects formed of space and movement and thrown in these two components, in short, this naturalism results from this shift from machines built for local needs to the global and round machine of the world.

The world is modelled on the clock, where time is counted in a reversible way. This timepiece tells time but is not subjected to it; and it even prevents the conception of a different time. The astronomical pocket clock is an automaton for which the circulation of planets becomes, conversely, the giant model. Newton enters France through Voltaire, as we know, and triumphs through Laplace. He conquers celestial and general mechanics, astronomy and physics. The idea of a long span of time, necessary for transformism and evolutionism, could never have emerged from this mechanistic or 'naturalist' context. The most determined adversaries of this duration – long, to be sure, but especially irreversible – were recruited amongst the mechanists, including Newtonians, partisans of reversible time, who represented the most well-informed party.

Thus, for a long time, the natural sciences remained exterior to their movement. In them the beast-machine theory remains marginal. La Fontaine's famous *Address to Madame de La Sablière* expresses, after Montaigne's *Apology*, the opinion of the throng of specialists who, like their rural contemporaries for centuries, opted for the soul of animals: Cureau de La Chambre, Gassendi, Bernier, Bayle, Leibniz, Charles Bonnet, Boullier, Fontenelle, La Mettrie, even if his animal soul becomes material, Renouvier himself …

Fabre? … Most of them, recently published in the collection *Corpus des œuvres de philosophie en langue française* and listed in the corresponding journal, together form an overwhelming majority. Animists? Diderot did indeed believe in primitive sensitive matter.

The fractal in the car cemetery

Leibniz, initiator of the infinitesimal world and of infinitesimal calculus, speaks fractal for the very first time: an animal, he says, is a machine of machines in its smallest parts. This proposition is all the more fascinating in that today we find its quasi-application in living organisms, whose cells and molecules fulfil sophisticated functions. Nanotechnologies, already?

Do those developing the mechanistic model think about what we do when we build a machine? Hands never make anything from nothing. They need what metaphysicians call prime matter: wood, bronze, brass, plastic, and so on. The balance wheel of a watch is characterised by its form, to be sure – thin, long, gravitational, etc. – but also by its material, usually an alloy. For everything, Aristotle, already, distinguished its matter and its form. But this alloy, being an artificial form, mixes materials; and this brass, this elinvar, contains crystals, molecules, atoms, and so forth, which means thousands of forms. Will we one day know how to descend in this way the scale of sizes to the point of making a machine sufficiently similar to the 'real' to encounter only forms down to the indefinably small? Have we ever made or even conceived of a machine that would remain a machine to that point? Leibniz' statement and miniaturisation question the mechanism in its depth.

Knowing the history of sciences, we have reason to laugh at the idea, since those who take as a model the computer – which one and from which generation? – forget that their predecessors drew, for their part, on what quickly became, with the help of progress, the junkyard of cars or the cemetery of locomotives. Time quickly renders these utensils outmoded. The watch from the classical period seems a wobbly trinket to us and Vaucanson's Duck has the appearance of a disarticulated museum piece. The mechanism accumulates in its wake the flea market of amusing old knickknacks. If nature imitates the mechanism, would it become this junkyard as quickly? Perhaps!

Automata

When we describe the behaviour of a mechanism – a clock or robot – as automatic, we still do not know what we are saying. To us, an automaton works without any subjective will or intention involved. It even becomes the perfect image of the naturalist divorce.

The fact is, the semantic family to which the word automaton refers has an old Indo-European root – *men* – that designates, to the contrary, mental activity: vehe-ment, de-mented, com-mentary, men-tion, mem-ory, mon-ument, de-mon-stration, mon-ey … we find here the formats mentioned before reappearing! The French term, *mon-tre,* for watch is itself from this root! The word that designates it says that it has a mind! And so we use a word that speaks of mental activity for a thing that we see as lacking it! The automaton has the same old relationship with mental activity as the Greeks had with gnomon and knowledge (see *A History of Scientific Thought: Elements of a History of Science*). The axis of the sundial, the gnomon, literally means 'one who knows'. In the end, we talk about what we call naturalism with words that contradict it and overtly say the opposite, that an intelligence exists that is less artificial than objective or objectal. An animist word!

Thing, object, real, automaton, watch … did the naturalist divorce ever exist?

Paradoxically, it did not start within the natural sciences – as we have seen from our visits above to totemist classes, animist physics, analogist mathematics and so on – but, on the contrary, with the birth of human sciences, including the aforementioned law. This carefully thought-out separation certainly allowed the study of cultures to constitute itself as soft in comparison with the hard sciences. To emerge and to develop, especially within the University. To my astonished eyes, the social sciences were born in France by ministerial decree. Or rather, their very birth precipitated the advent of the distinction between nature, the sole 'object' of hard sciences, and cultures, as a diversified field open to knowledge. Did naturalism engender human sciences or was it the other way around? Is the question decidable? If it is, it may well be only for the law, which alone has the right to decide on the supreme instance of decision. Detached, at any rate, from their old scientific matrix, the human sciences could at last, in their thus defined area, explore fields, forge their own methods and their singular objects, and at last dream of theories.

The drift thereby produced between the two continents of knowledge prompted two attitudes in the new sciences, in relation to the confrontation with the old sciences. Initially fascinated, the new sciences strove to mimic their elders; then, to the contrary, ignorance of the latter and even aggressiveness toward them prevailed and continues to astonish today. I know nothing authentically naturalist aside from university classifications, with their absurd divisions bent on separating the hard and the soft sciences, and amongst students, the uncultured educated from the ignorant cultured. The bridging by the Instructed Third remains a utopia.

In this regard, I note a difference in rhythm between the French and German universities. Auguste Comte's classification was the first to prevail in the 19th century, whereupon sociology joined the list of the sciences, alongside physics and biology. This discipline – invented by Comte (both the name and the thing), subsequently classified among the human sciences, proceeded from those that take the sky or living organisms as objects of study. Comte knew no hiatus between the sciences of nature and those that treat the collective, nor did he impose any. To the contrary, sociology appeared, in the classification, to present a continuity with mechanics or anatomy. If, for him, the study of societies follows from other disciplines, humans dissociate themselves little from the external world and, insofar as the social becomes naturalised, naturalism recedes. It recedes all the more in that, as nobody wants to read the second Auguste Comte, who was religious as all hell, they venerate him as the ancestor of today's 'positivisms,' which he is not in any way, shape or form. In writing these lines, I realise that the effort of *The Troubadour of Knowledge* itself, prior to *The Natural Contract*, and their double bridging, in opposition to the naturalist formatting, emerged in all likelihood from this French-language tradition.

In contrast, scientific classifications, of which there were many in the late 19th century amongst our German friends of the likes of Rickert, upheld this now common separation because they promoted the sciences of mind (*Geisteswissenschaften*), or rather those of cultures, and defended their dignity alongside, and often against, the dignity we are accustomed to granting to the long-established, exact sciences. They did so all the more because, for the first time and against the universalism of the Enlightenment, these classifiers gave several precise and concrete definitions of culture or rather of cultures, inspired as they were by the defence and illustration of the particularism of local communities. Germany was then defending local culture against French universalist humanism. How odd to observe the development of a university institution preparing the naturalist divorce, when it was barely emerging from a romanticism that was animist through and through!

Thereafter, and in all latitudes, ethnology or anthropology, in short, the human sciences refined these definitions and adopted them. In the same period, American universities developed little by little under strong German influence; we can find still today a great many traces of this hold. Their culturalism of the time, and their multiculturalism of today remain of distant Germanic inspiration. The French university system, in its turn, did not escape this model, at least starting with Renan and *The Future of Science*, in which the author promises this future to philology.

Insofar as this naturalism is embodied, consecrated and spread by the academic institution, it descends directly from the historic moment when the German university was radiating throughout the world and imposing its seal on it. Are we to conclude that we are dealing here with nothing but an artefact?

No doubt. For I have never read a writer, no less a poet, or heard a composer, inspired by this naturalism. Neither have I seen a discovery of any importance in the so-called hard sciences that can be said to proceed from the distinction between nature and culture. This separation between a part that is smooth, flat, dull, unified and one that is proliferating would tend rather to neutralise scientific invention and development. Invented by Descartes, this led to what Leibniz called a 'novel of physics,' whereas his quite analogist critique invented our modernity in nearly all disciplines.

As much as I believe the classifications of natural history to be totemist in nature, the contemporary sciences of information to be animist, and mathematics quasi-analogist, and, in all three cases, I understand, in this light, the origins of these disciplines and part of their development, I also see naturalism being born as a pedagogical artefact, not only favourable to the emergence of human sciences, but, by its overly simplistic and repetitive character, useful for education, exercise and transmission. Here, indeed, are *the best possible formats for the mimetic passion;* and without mimicry and mimesis, neither learning nor teaching is possible. Institutions live as children of mimicry.

Invention requires something else: a conversion. Far be it from me to advise anyone to *convert to* totemism, *to* animism or *to* any other worldview; this book simply provides types of departures, diverse ways of camping elsewhere, of leaving the campus. But, in absolute terms, it is better to *convert*, change looks, bodies, thinking, language, hopes, standards, throw one's sandals into the fire, have no fear of going alone and naked, pitch one's tent in the forest of the real, endure contempt, not to give in to vainglory. It's necessary but not enough. Because one also needs to be fortunate enough to come upon the right problem at exactly the right time. This double adventure turns the inventor into a suffering alien, a tormented stranger, both rare. The art of inventing is said in an exotic language; our geniuses come from elsewhere, from Amazonia, Australia, the New Hebrides, etc.

Having come from 'nature', they make a new culture emerge. Here it is at last.

One: mine and dead

Pig cooking in winter; rogations in spring when the priest blessed the fields; the implacable rivalry between local factions: the Red and the White; the calf fairs right outside the front door and the poultry markets on Sundays; the subtle mosaic of Occitan tongues from Béarn to Périgord and from the Landes to Catalonia – these are some of the cultures from where I, an aborigine, come. My friends from the Aber-Benoît, from Niedermorschwihr, from Molines-en-Queyras and from Méhun-sur-Yèvre had their own variations in Breton, Alsatian, Piedmontese or Berrichon. Destroyed by the demise of the rural population, decimated by the two world war butcheries and the green revolutions in the countryside, wiped out by urbanisation, highways, tour operators, television and more, these rural cultures have left nothing but a few ruins here and there of interest to no one but ethnologists.

Two, three: ours and ailing

When I hear the lines, '*Mourir pour sa patrie est un si digne sort, / Qu'on briguerait en foule une si belle mort*' ('Tis so worthy to die for one's country/ Who would not court so bright a destiny'), I wonder who wrote such horrors, even though not long ago I thought Pierre Corneille's *Horace* the masterpiece, if not of the human mind, at least of our second culture.

The shadow of which I still carry within me, without regretting its disappearance. Here, again, are some of its features. Composed of a solid expertise in Latin and Greek most definitely, in Hebrew and Sanskrit if necessary, it reaches back in time to the confines of history, toward the beginning of writing. It travels in space from a singular place where the first sense of culture was defined – as the set of singular practices of a group, the rurality of Gascony in my case – to the other language of France, the Oïl, its history, its literature, its artworks and so on, and to a number of neighbouring countries where people speak Spanish, Italian, English, German or Russian, languages with analogous works. Add to this a solid knowledge of the history of science, pagan myths and monotheist theology, and you have sketched the silhouette, in profile, as our humanists, from Erasmus and Montaigne to Romain Rolland and Stefan Zweig, sculpted it in themselves and spread it around themselves, with me receiving it and attempting, for the first time in vain, to perpetuate its shape. Be it through Greek geometry, the epistles of St. Paul and human rights, it tended, as I have said, to see itself as universal, at once in the abstract and for the individual. Subsequently, we feared that it was only Europe's.

The honest man after my heart travelled, *thirdly*, from Oc in the Occident, that is from pig cooking, the local, to the Louvre, the CNRS and UNESCO, the global, during his adolescence, to return, serene and wrinkled, from Euclid and Plutarch, to rurality. The greatest in the rejoicing of my soul united their journey out with their return: Cervantes, drunk on books, on Panza's donkey; Montaigne to Lahontan; and Diderot, on Jacques's horse, under the pitchforks.

Four: theirs

Recently, the redefinition of what my society means, *fourthly,* by culture has driven these shadows into labyrinths with no entry or exit, with the result that that the three preceding 'mines' have disappeared. Here, once again, are some of the features. I'm not very familiar, I confess, with the names and works of those who have taken the place of Mistral and Racine, of Ravel and the Rogations, all the singers, animators, administrators in the ministry in charge, industrial and banking sponsors, idols of political and media show business, whose images are widely disseminated.

I enjoy the redistribution of the sciences, of music and of data on the Web, the new interactive sharing that threatens the stars, quickly stale though still fresh and, no doubt, the very system of cultural exceptions, since in the end no difference distinguishes the radio journalist, the news anchor, the priest in the pulpit and the university professor in the classroom. All hold forth on a channel with no interaction; all sole owners of access to sources of knowledge or information; all champions obliging their contemporaries' bodies to abandon themselves to the slouching posture of passengers, while the computer straightens them into the active arc of conducturs: the body never deceives.

Concerning this double redefinition that causes the Academy to regress from first to last place, I feel no outrage or jealousy at the unstable fortune, power and renown of those who benefit from it. So be it. I live with my time and do not find it so bad for all that. Vulgar, violent and deadly, no doubt, but rather less so than other periods, for it no longer produces, as far as I can count, tens of millions of deaths like the previous one, that of my childhood, which, for its part, was armed with this second culture whose memory I still carry in my blood.

I enjoy, on the contrary, the triple gap Occitan-Academy-media, by which I mean *local-abstract universal-global expansion*, and the way this disequilibrium, inside me, opens the way, I hope, to clear-sightedness. There will be no turning back. What's more, I rejoice to see, moving forward, the outlines of a fifth profile, which is this.

Five: human, generic and natural

Under the gentle pressure of ethnology, the earlier spatial limits of Occitan and the Occident became more flexible; through it we learnt about the cultures of peoples with no writing, excluded from history by the sovereign decision of history to use writing to date itself. While oral traditions outnumbered the writing exception, the latter took no interest in reducing the numerical fracture for several millennia. Crossing more than the sharp frontier marked, since Pascal, by the Pyrénées, we now travel not only from lexicon to lexicon, but amongst tribes of tradition without translation. A hundred civilisations, unknown not so long ago, are being revived and valued. Practicing, thanks to these truly human sciences, a new form of knowledge and hence of tolerance, we respect them. Better still, and this book testifies to this, they open us to humbly revisiting our own. First act, so much for space, more *disparate* and closer than we imagine. But we are witnessing a second act, even more decisive. Concerning duration.

Under the pressure of all the hard sciences, the temporal boundaries of my second culture prove to be oddly narrow. Its so-called universality is, at best, five thousand years old. The new culture, the fifth, at last natural, counts fifteen billion of them. The chronological background against which our children are cultivated today is deepening to the point that the patch that we cultivated not so long ago seems bafflingly small. To arrive at an extension where the mind finally breathes in the wide-open sea, these hard sciences happened upon a simple discovery, almost in unison. They all recently invented methods of dating; each discipline managed to plunge its objects into a time punctuated by precision-measured stages. Everything can be dated and can even date itself. The things of the universe and of the world, living organisms and people, exist, together, as places of memory that we arrogantly believe belong to us alone or that we alone know how to create. Whence the development of a chronology in which things themselves and knowledge of them emerge, change and disappear; whence the gradual and once again *disparate* constitution of what I've called the Great Story: uncertain and contingent when it is moving forward, like all stories, through spectacular turns of events and mutations, it comes to have a certain order when it is told in retrospect.

In this way we can recount it thanks to another simple discovery that is related to the first: one after another, all the sciences found that *the things around us write as much and better than we do* – they even read, at times – so that knowledge consists in deciphering the thousand and one codes with which things, inert or living, engraved their own languages, by themselves and on themselves, *en soi et pour soi*. In the past, small stories of small-scale history were told on the basis of written texts in a narrow group of languages; the Great Story today is coded in multiple alphabets, not necessarily human, and marvellously ancient: in cosmic radiation, galactic blobs, black holes, falling meteorites, rock magnetism, tectonic plates, cliff strata, Cambrian limestone, Lucy's fossilised pelvis, molecule folds, and the DNA of species. In all, but also in us, this story is written. We read it and feel the full force of *the blow delivered by the hard sciences to our narcissisms: we are not the only ones to speak or write; all things in the world do so*. Suddenly, they enter our home. Our ancient cultures opposed cultures *with* writing and nature *without* writing; the new one welcomes cultures *without* writing and nature *with* writing. A new confluent.

Just as vernacular, national or global history supported, with its temporal and spatial structures, the two cultures facing extinction, so the Great Story supports the new culture with thousands of circumstances of colossal duration. Humans do not find themselves in it confronted with a strange or absurd world; rather they are born and live by its evolution. In the old culture, knowledge excluded stories; in the current one, this story includes all knowledge. In this way the things of nature enter the house of cultures. There is but one habitat now.

Peace in the conflict between faculties: henceforth not only do we celebrate the chaotic and contingent expansion of periods of time or the multicoloured and mosaic federation of spaces, we also drink to the nuptials, unexpected in our universities, of the sciences and the arts, whose divorce will prove to be a short-lived, foolish interlude in our history. On one hand, scientists have acquired techniques that used to be called humanist: they read, decode, date and recount; they pay for this entry into culture with a novel mix of chance and necessity. On the other, historians, changing memory, have acquired an huge expanse of time whose projection on their time changes even their objects. Just as scholars read Greek, Arabic or Chinese characters, a hundred languages, and hence a hundred ways of knowing, so scientists decipher a hundred languages too: the coloured bands of spectrography, the alpha or beta molecule folds, the arithmetic language of simple bodies, the four letters of genetics. To each discipline, its language, its local code, *belongs not only to the speciality, as it did long ago and recently still, but to the things themselves.*

As different and varied as the regions of the world from which they originate, these languages describe, in return, a madly multitudinous sky, a madly complex Earth, madly varied landscapes, madly implicated bodies. Multiplicities invade the simplistic old schemas, henceforth saturated with singularities. An underlying diversity characterises nature as well as cultures. These varieties, branching in space and in languages, correspond to the chaotic contingency in the time of the story, so named for its unpredictable bifurcations and its surprising mutations. Hence the new style of these sciences, once known as hard, their appearance now more detailed than general, more rugged than smooth, more branching than simplified, more individuated than abstract, more information processing than a geometrician, at once better, worse and, in any case, more informed on the Web than in libraries – in short, more procedural than declarative. *Historiated*, the real answers our *historiated* modes of knowledge on the Web. Thus our cognitive age leans more toward disparate individuals than to the simplicity of classes, more toward singularities than to concepts. Hence the shift down toward a ramified story rather than up to laws. The old square – schemas, principles, classes, the excellent exception of expertise – finds itself overwhelmed by the new quadrilateral – landscapes, stories, individuals, the diluvial multiplicity of information available on the Web. On the side of nature, the simplicity of naturalism disappears.

Generic culture

As novel for spaces as for periods of time, this fifth culture then becomes properly *generic*, that is *proper to the species*. Formed from the plurality of coded things – inert, vital or human – it cannot disregard the particularisms of the preceding cultures, attached as they were, one to Quercy or to Guyenne, the other to the Mediterranean or to the West ... but it pleasantly mocks what some arrogantly called the inhabited world. Though contingent and variegated, it leads nonetheless to the idea that our very differences contribute to composing, over time, a common story: *common to the people and to the things of the world*; the whole universe, they and us included, descend, trembling with surprise, from a possible or probable big bang; the Earth and life come, no doubt, from the burning accretion and from the cooling of planets. And here is the continuation of the story: after *Homo erectus*, *Homo sapiens* emerged in Africa and stayed there. According to this scenario, which seems likely today, the whole thing can be told like a children's tale: crossing the Suez some hundred thousand years ago, some humans spread out across the planet where climate constraints, food sources and the diverse relations that they invented on occasion conditioned the diversity that we observe today. How? We know only bits and pieces of this story, through the opaqueness of the millenia. But, with respect to cultures, the complexity of naturalism is very much diminished.

Because Coppens-like paleoanthropologists are now leapfrogging on the backs of Lévi-Strauss-like ethnologists, generic culture plunges these differences into a common story that straddles them with its contingent unity. Where earlier cultures raised walls, this one begins to build bridges, fragile and flexible. There is, of course, a chaotic mosaic of exceptions, but the Great Story of the wanderings of *Homo sapiens* attempts to develop them over a duration quivering with bifurcations. *Viator*, it never stops crossing over to both sides of boundaries and thus brings to life, in retroaction, a common world, things and humans together; over the highest mountains and the widest seas, this story and its predecessors have never stopped opening passes and traveling across straights, already travelled, on the occasion of such and such a circumstance, by their great-grandparents. So I resume the story. *Erectus*, then *Sapiens,* from this side of the Pyrénées, crossed to the other side; having set out from this side of the Suez first, they arrived on the other, in Eurasia; having reached this side of the Arafura sea, *Sapiens* travelled, some sixty thousand years ago, to the other side, to the shores of Australia; then, having arrived on this side of the Bering, they landed, some twenty thousand years ago, on the other side, in Alaska, before descending to the Rockies and the Andes. Note: I am telling a probable story, subject to rectifications. Note: the scenarios can vary, the form of the narrative remains the same. *Did this contingent time produce, at least in part, the variegated space of cultures formed in its passage?* A truth mixed with doubts – which is to say, precisely, a story – corresponds to this duration and this expanse. As in any mosaic, the generic silhouette, in a vast and chaotic time, crosses the boundaries of pieces broken by the old puzzle formed by thousands of boundaries. Does the time of the Great Story play the part of stem cell for the diversity of cultures?

I do not doubt that thousands of literary, artistic and philosophical inspirations will well up from this Great Story, as from a new source. Invariant for all and once formulated, it can be heard anywhere, in any language; or it can be taught, in vernacular languages, from the New Hebrides to Lapland, or learnt in scholarly languages, in the lecture halls of the Sorbonne or Stanford. I proposed the programme for this in the final pages of *The Incandescent*. The swell of its temporal flows licks the shores of space, even up to the Pyrenean crests, dear to Blaise Pascal; it draws its source from the story of the Universe, follows vital evolution and *is received in universal language*. Again I mean by this not a unique language, but rather a hundred translations that can be heard and understood by a thousand and one people; depending on how much detail is sought, everyone can participate, telling it or hearing it, in the regional dialect-specialist jargon duo. I can express it quickly, as above, for my grandchildren, in comic strips, while others expatiate on technical evidence, which they examine in detail in difficult articles.

A new space corresponds to a new time

Finally, I do not doubt that the new information and communication technologies that I was speaking of earlier are already giving an elective support to this fifth culture, just as, to put it quickly, human writing, invented some three millennia ago, did for the second culture, and non-interactive media for the fourth. Their speed of execution is almost commensurate with the old economy of thought that abstraction permitted. We are living in a century of Light, of its clarity, but, also, in addition, of its speed. Thanks to mathematics, the concept of circle allows us to conceive in one go of an infinite number of round objects; conversely, to better grasp in one go millions of round forms, we use this abstract circle that I've termed declarative. Just as electronics now allows us to enjoy the individual longer without constantly bypassing the concrete with schemas, so culture takes on the procedural, branching, detailed, landscape style that I've described. This too it owes to the computer.

Whose techniques immerse us, moreover, in a space as new as the time in which dating makes us live. Just think of the meaning of the *address*. The usual one of the post refers to Cartesian-type coordinates and to a distance measured as much by geometry as by outdated politics: it indicates the country, the city, the street, a number. Now the fact is that nothing noteworthy comes to us anymore through the postal service. Messages reach us on cell phones or by email, with addresses in letter or numbers, in short in a code – like all things in the world – with no further reference to some form of measured space. Foolishly, people everywhere repeat that distances have thereby been reduced, as if we were still living in a space where getting somewhere by bicycle or plane instead of walking and swimming shortened the distance travelled. No, the internet and the cell phone transfer our lives and relations into a space unrelated to the old space. Geometers would say: in the old days of networks, we lived in a Euclidian, Cartesian, metrical space, that of portolan charts and *mappa mundi*, of terrestrial or celestial globes, whereas today we haunt a topological space, without distance or measure, no longer that of surveyors, but that of Riemann and of colourists.

The word *address* also, and by its origin, *rex*, *rectus*, refers to the king and to rights in law (*droit*): the police and the tax collector could find, in this way, the dens where lawbreakers and delinquent taxpayers were hiding. The change that I'm describing did not take *place* in the same metrics, with new distances relative to the same references, as when we used to move to a new place, but rather it made us truly change space. We leapt into topology. What becomes of the law (*droit*), when the straight (*droite*) line becomes homeomorphic to a serpentine shape and the sphere to a Phrygian cap? We then see another type of police, other jurisprudences, a new system of government, along with the obsolescence of the regime of parties and representatives appearing on the horizon. An emerging culture entails unexpected politics.

Lastly, the practice of reference does not only concern habitable or politicised space, but also knowledge, among other things. In the past, expertise played on access; scientists, scholars and historians enjoyed an elective knowledge of sources from having spent time in laboratories, universities and libraries, with good books, groups of colleagues, and so on, blithely accumulating footnotes and bibliographies – the defensive armour and shield of the serious expert who recopies. Well referenced, a good book cites good addresses. That expertise just died at the same time that the university is going through its death throes. Search engines, working in topological space, are replacing them, where the old scholar traversing metrical space would take the shortest route by train or by plane to consult the catalogue of a rare library. As exhausted as the stars from which we still receive light but which astrophysics shows have long been extinct, our institutions still oblige students to take the costly train to go to crowded lecture halls to receive, often quite poorly, knowledge that is available, in overabundance, from their homes, for free, on the Web.

Open to the species, generic culture opens a time common to the geneses of people and things in the world and is transported toward another, qualitative space, in which we now live, with these things, though philosophy and politics have not fully grasped the novelty of this. Its topology having digested contingency, as the duration of hominisation had done, its variegated colours exalt the body and landscapes.

Landscapes, indeed. First for the body. Since I'm speaking of time, this is its age. Based on the civil registry and demographic statistics, I estimate its expectancy today at less than a century. I'm trying, however, to calculate its duration better by dating it with the precision acquired earlier. If the language we speak strengthened knowledge and the arts over the last four centuries, and even over the three millennia during which there were exchanges amongst its ancestors, our arches, for their part, toughened in the course of the wanderings of our ancestors from the time they left Africa, some hundred thousand years ago; our knee joint formed between the pelvic movements of Lucy, newly descended to the savanna, and our hike only yesterday, over about three million years; underneath our recent cerebral circumvolutions lie reptilian layers that evoke hundreds of millions of years; the DNA and the molecules that our cells manufacture started to duplicate some three billion, eight hundred million years ago when life appeared on our planet; but the atoms that compose them, nitrogen and carbon, were forged in the furnace of cooling galaxies more than ten billion years ago. In plunging from our organs into their components, a chronometer sinks through our body with gradations that correspond quite well, detail by detail, to the periods of the Universe, to the formation of the Earth around us and the evolution of the living things that wander through our environment. The past of our bodies goes back past not only our birth and those of our close relatives, but also the thinness of the history learnt in school, of the writing and words from preceding cultures. Yet, nothing is closer or more concrete than our bodies. We ignore the age of its components and the existence, in it, of temporal strata as thick as those of the things themselves. Here are proportions, here is a harmony, unsuspected only yesterday. Dating my age enables me to evaluate the oldness of my body and that of these things, both forgotten, but especially their congruence. My age follows the time of their association. Not only do things circulate amidst us and live in our home, but they plunge into me to make my body. Not only does my thinking understand, albeit with difficulty, this span of time, but, formed of elements born with the universe, or constituted, slowly and contingently, with our planet, accompanying also the evolution of the living, my body is rooted in it and lives from it. Here we have three sites of memory with synchronous details. My environment is made up of things that make up my body: they descend from the same age. Here I am discovering a new *Umwelt*: or, better still, here are the hyphens of being-in-the-world materialised. I don't know about being, I don't know about the world, but the details of my body follow from their relations. Tremendously archaic and yet new, the body of the new culture finds in it the archaic world tremendously.

Let us correct Blaise Pascal: neither space nor time engulfs my body; they probe it, they form it, they measure it, they scan it even better than my thinking, which is often lost in the difficult intuition of such durations. No, the universe does not crush me, some of its details run through me. Conversely, my many decades of spring interlace these same objective details and, thereby singularise and subjectivise them. Humanising numerous details of what was called inhuman nature, this fifth culture gives rise to a new *Hominescent*. Will it sign the Natural Contract? Better: it embodies it, in itself.

Learning these things leads us to rewrite history. Now, then, for its landscapes. We Westerners pride ourselves, sometimes with good reason, on our taste for exploration. Curious as we are, we love changing horizons. Who has ever seen a ship from another culture landing on the shores of Europe to visit us? Conversely, ever since Ulysses, at least, set off to known and unknown seas and worlds, our ancestors have never ceased from plotting daring circuits on the world map: Pytheas from Marseille to the north, Vasco de Gama to the south, Marco Polo to the east, Christopher Columbus and Jacques Cartier to the west, without forgetting the journey of Hanno around Africa or Livingston and Stanley, who separately followed in the tracks of Arab tour operators of the period through the savanna and the forest of Africa. More or less daring, these explorers described a number of exotic countries, and told of their first encounters with the naturals, the indigenous or aborigines, even the savages; in short, the creatures with bodies and strange religions and customs. These cultural shocks did not always take place without violence; fear, often legitimate, hatred and contempt, less understandable, and exploitation and crime, unpardonable, got in the way.

In short, alterity was at play; differences ever and again. A question haunted the words and minds of these explorers: Who would one meet in the course of these travels? Men and woman, truly? Really like us? Imbued as we are now with ethnology, ethics and political correctness, we have become proud, belatedly to be sure, of teaching, if not practicing, tolerance. But the question subsisted. Now, for the first time, we have an answer, albeit vague: provided with DNA dated in the same way, American Indians, Aboriginal peoples of Australia, Eskimos, Fuegians, Inuits, Armagnacs and Burgundians, we all descend from the small group of *Sapiens* who left Africa some hundred thousand years ago, according to the scenario that my expert colleagues deem probable. Our explorer ancestors and we travellers ourselves only ever encounter cousins, whose culture, body and skin diverge as a result of hard environmental constraints, temporal and local. We have no need any longer for morality or a highly legal and solemnly proclaimed text to believe that we are brothers. We now know it. This will not necessarily bring us peace, since everywhere there is burning hatred between enemy twins, but at least we can erase from history the term *encounter* and replace it with *reunion*. Ah, we haven't seen each other for millennia! No wonder we don't look alike! Do you remember our common parents? No wonder we look alike!

If, by a new time count, our body changes its view of the world, this recent result also transforms our erroneous view of man and of our history. *Who are we? Where do we come from?* These old philosophical questions, which, long ago and recently still, were unanswerable, and so hard to document that many of us, discouraged, stopped asking, now finds solutions, temporary, to be sure, since they rely on the current state of research, but placed in a process of inquiry in which their probability increases, decreases, is continually managed and they can at least be recounted, in the form of a story. Having originated in Africa, we have no doubt been chasing after globalisation for a hundred thousand years. Travelling today over four continents, we reunite with brothers and sisters; returning to the first continent, we find ourselves with mothers and fathers.

Our history was mistaken. Will we rewrite it? The explorers were not traveling straight ahead, they were returning. History, to be sure, but also ethnology, lacked the chronological background. Common ancestors are revealed through the Great Story of our emergence and our wanderings about the globe. The hominisation of our migrating and globalised species scattered us everywhere, from a probable source, stem or cradle, situated, and this is something that is passionately debated and will be for a long time to come, somewhere around the Kenyan Rift, toward the Great Lakes, perhaps toward Chad, in any case somewhere in the centre of Africa. We stayed there for millions of years, then slowly emigrated toward 'the Cape', to the south, and Egypt, to the north, and finally left the continent and spread out in all latitudes.

New scenario: If I camp out in the vicinity of the polar circle in the midst of Inuits or a tribe of Australians, I now find the courage within me to approach them smiling and say, 'Delighted to see you again. Do you recall, we parted ways sixty or a hundred thousand years ago?' In fact, I spent long evenings in the vicinity of Alice Springs telling this story to Aborigines who burst out with laughter to hear a European at last singing myths of treks, like they do. They would answer me, 'This we have always known, we who say that in a primeval time, that we call *Dreaming*, strange living beings spread everywhere, creating things and relations.' And greeted in Africa with even more outbursts of laughter, I try to say, 'Have you found me much changed since millions of years ago?' '*Toubab*, our great grandson,' they reply. I brought them my new book, for them to smile at it.

Plunging our bodies, our intentions and our groups into a new space, generic culture awakens the gigantic memory of the things in the world, of the living, of others, of me, of my body. Who are we? Disparate and total parts of evolution. Individual selves and a we that these stories assemble, in the midst of the things.

I know. You don't like science. What do the big bang, tectonic plates, Lucy and DNA have to do with us, with our matters of love, death and politics? I hear you. You advise me to engage in serious business, those in the news, written, oral or visual, where we find the philosopher's morning prayer; you say I should participate in the noisy spectacle of the presidential elections and of the latest bus burning. Nothing in the Great Story, you insist, developed with bravado and, what's more, only chaotic and probable, either consoles us or keeps us from not getting along because we do not speak the same language, from hating each other because we do not practice the same religion, from exploiting the weak, from persecuting others in various ways, and so on. I hear you and you are right. But forgive me: although founded on the horror of the Trojan war or the prohibition of human sacrifice under the fist of Abraham, the father of monotheisms, did the old culture, whose loss I hear lamented everywhere, ever deliver us from these daily violences throughout history, of the massacres of the Gauls, the Indians, the Cathars or the Aborigines, of Auschwitz or Hiroshima?

I know. Sciences do not impart meaning; only cultures announce it. How, then, can we answer these painful questions, varying endlessly, about the problem of evil, which leaves us inconsolable? How can we work on peace, the highest collective good of all? You are right, through culture. Which? Being that the preceding one is gone and the current one is vain, given over to flashiness, we must invent a new one, which, at the very least, would separate humans less and connect them to the things of the world. A generic culture? We have here at least the beginnings of it, the space, time and air that it will breathe.

When will politics realise that citizens today were all born from the Natural Contract? Equipped as it is with always soft sciences, when will it integrate a little hard knowledge so as to acquire this generic culture and understand at last the world in which we live, at the least for the last fifty years, at the most for billions of years?

If you do not like the sciences, perhaps you do like the things of a world whose dated details run through your flesh as they do mine? Politics, the old human sciences and academic culture hardly concern themselves with this, as if we were living alone, *in camera* or between humans, in the public greenhouses of cities, facing the pure spectacle of combats, facing the pure combat of spectacles, indifferent to a nature that has become external, massive, unitary and opaque through the blindness of our practices. In response to this disinterest, it has been exacting revenge, it seems, for decades, and, in a few more, its vengeance will be more deadly still.

Here we have an amiable hominid culture departing, on the contrary, from the things of the world to return to them. Like us. Nuptials of nature and culture.

Stems

Have I been dreaming? Some writers, scientists and philosophers in the West are testifying to such exotic views or religions that you'd think they were hunters in the forest or bedecked with feathers. Although their attitudes are as disparate as the colours of a Harlequin cloak, can they nonetheless be assembled, like those colours, superimposed, that end up composing the light that whitens Pierrot's costume? The preface to this book speaks of stem cells that contain, in both a real and virtual way, the sum total of others: nerve, blood, bone, etc. I am dreaming again of importing this sum into philosophy.

Catholic composition

Here is a very different example of such a stem assemblage that succeeds, in a way, at this type of addition. It seems to me that the name of the Catholic religion – καθ–όλον, *catholon*, means universal in Greek – is coherent from this standpoint. I do not deny that other rites or religions may exist about which the same thing could be said, but my ignorance, in this regard, outweighs my expertise.

The Acts of the Apostles relate the event that took place at Pentecost with a genuinely *animist* image of a breath or, better yet, a violent wind that filled the place where the apostles were sitting and whose fire made them speak in tongues, to the Parthians, to the Medes, to those living in Mesopotamia, in Judea, in Cappadocia, in Pontus and in Asia, in Phrygia and in Pamphylia, in Egypt and in Libya, to immigrants, to Jews and to converts to Judaism, Cretans and Arabs – a list that would not seem out of place in an ethnology treatise. Animism, once again: previously only visible to a donkey and to a few rare inspired prophets, myriads of angels fly by, sing and disappear in silence, on the night of Christmas in the populated sky.

As for the incarnate person of Jesus, born that night, how can his double body, his double nature, at once human and divine, be described, other than as *fetishist*? A fetish is usually presented as the fusion of two living beings, on the one hand, but also as sculpted by the hand of man and representing a divinity. The Portuguese word from which this fetish is derived means both fabricated or factitious, and magical or holy, like a fairy. *Fait* or *fée*? Fabricated or fairy? No doubt both! At any rate, an object that speaks, since fairy derives from the Latin *fari*, which also means speak. That we behave and think like fetishists nowadays, when we live surrounded by fabricated objects that speak, be they telephones or computers, that much is obvious. But that the Christian Incarnation designates a body coming from a woman's womb and bearing the word – *Et* verbum *caro* factum *est* – there we have something even more astonishing!

And what are we to make of the four gospels that tradition has bequeathed us, three times, at least, symbolised in the form of a lion, an ox and an eagle? What are we to think of this bestiary that decorates churches, which finds no source in the writings of the evangelists, thusly associated with their doubles? How many saints and statues of saints are, likewise, represented alongside an animal or a plant: their *totem*? For in the practice of images and the veneration of saints, rejected by monotheisms anterior and posterior to Catholicism, in the multiple stories depicted in the masses of paintings and sculptures that invade cathedrals and small country chapels, who would not see a reprise, against all informed criticism, an often wild rehashing of the ancient myths of *paganism*? Worse, when a city, a community, a brotherhood or a corporation assigns itself a patron saint or other heavenly protector, how could one help thinking, again, of some *totem*?

Ever since we were instructed to love our neighbour as ourselves and to save our own souls, ever since the autobiography of Saint Paul and the *Confessions* of Saint Augustine, authentic individuals have taken to peopling the planet, little by little, with their irreducible originality; which is another name for an *analogical* culture, in which everyone decides for himself, takes care of himself, survives and saves himself, autonomous, personal, different, free … bridging these singularities by transcendent relations: a communion of saints … Who could finally decide once and for all between the strict *monotheism* and the true *polytheism* of this religion, given that it teaches a Trinity that is one and triple at once?

Catholon: I am bird, see my wings; I am mouse, long live rats. Compact, capable of totality, Catholicism does not appear to decide between a hundred possible decisions described by the history of religions and practices, here and there, by various populations scattered all over the planet; Parthians, Medes, residents of Asia and Cappadocia … they each say it in *their* language. Ask Catholicism all the questions that would open it to one of the worldviews in the classification that has guided us, and it will always respond yes. It seems to me that the totality that its name signifies is intended not so much to address all humans in order to convert them, as, converted in itself and for itself, but to describe the span of its ritual traditions, as if it contained all religious possibilities, already there everywhere and spoken elsewhere in other languages, as if it *connected* them all, like a *stem* of sorts. Maybe other religions exist which could be honoured by the same description, but I bear witness to this one, since I know it best.

Time after time, hundreds of different buds burgeoned from its compact mass, from its soft womb, its pulp, its plasma, from the additivity combining its abilities, from the uncanny completeness of its mixes, in short, from this stem. For such choices to emerge, there must be a base, a bank from which to draw options. These choices, precisely, which it often condemned under the rigorous name of *heresies* – a Greek term meaning choices – decided on courses and plotted bifurcations on elective, tight, determined paths, more critical, better defined, thin, narrow, carved out, more exact and precise, more logical … frankly harder, purer, less charged with *accretions*, but also less capable of sustaining a global anthropology: razor-sharp paths or stalks burgeoning from a stem soft as virgin and mother.

The Catholic religion is also called Roman, less due its ecclesiastical origin in the Eternal City than to the accumulative nature of the paganism practiced in Rome from its founding to its fall. Victors, emperors, centurions and legionaries brought back the statues, idols or gods of their enemies, and put them in their sanctuaries, alongside their own, not regarding them as foreign or hateful, but rather as new auxiliaries. Here the religious adds, mixes, amalgamates, includes rather than excludes; indeed, it connects. It is often said that, unlike the paganisms of this type, monotheisms practice exclusion, logical and human. To be sure, Catholicism asks its flock to worship one God alone, but, Roman, it aspires nonetheless to inclusion, at least in its rituals and practices, no doubt to form a stem in the ancient and modern sense of the word. A bricolage, perhaps? But then, assembled systems tend, today, to catch up with and replace perfect systems. Reality evidences more of the relational than the rational. Will an ecumenical accretion, likewise, make peace between different religions?

By this sort of complete bank of dispersed details, does Catholicism symmetrise, in immanence – facts, behaviours, objects, diverse living beings, etc. – the mind of a transcendent God? Just as a single trunk precedes its branches, does it contain, before any decision, all of its heresies? 'Divine hodgepodge' was what the historian Ernest Lavisse called it. Stem, I say.

Such a person can, therefore, consider himself Catholic while practicing, blindly at least, totemism, animism, analogism and so forth. But there are others, like Einstein, a pantheist, Langevin, a materialist, Pasteur or Schrödinger, both spiritualists, Monod, an atheist, or still others, Jews, Protestants, Buddhists, or Muslims, who with no difficulty practice biochemistry, astronomy, physics or medicine and who can, furthermore, invent in those fields. These examples converge toward a stem that is compatible with distinctive practices of knowledge, that it in no way hinders and that it may even favour. Therein lies the promise of another sum of possible worldviews and of an ecumenical metaphysics.

The sciences say less than they do or they do more than they say. Their universal character is revealed not so much by their analytical or formal truth value, for this truth value, demonstrable or tested, is constantly changing across the ages, with new inventions and discoveries, as by pre-existing attitudes and views that are oddly compatible with them: like catholic, in the etymological sense. Who would not recognise a stem of sorts therein?

A summary of the book: Do some sciences entail naturalism? A hundred times, yes; no need for demonstration. And others totemism? Yes, again. And yet others animism or analogism? A thousand times yes. Can I generalise and conclude from this that all sciences are compatible with all worldviews?

More examples: the disputes on the European continent sparked by Newtonian attraction came from a perfectly rational reaction; could one believe in reactions at a distance without bowing to *animism*? Leibniz, the initiator of the notion of the dynamics of force, did not hesitate at all to reintroduce substantial units; his sensitive monads peopled the universe. Here was a prolific inventor: infinitesimal calculus, *analysis situs*, calculation of probabilities, dynamics, binary arithmetic, pre-relativity, calculator, pre-computing; in short, he was the initiator par excellence of the tissue that composes our contemporary sciences: everything in Leibniz comes from an ideology explicitly opposed to Cartesian naturalism. When Bergson speaks of the *élan vital* is he expressing a certain *vitalism*? For decades now contemporary sciences have been veering toward animism, and even more toward *analogism*: information theory, multiplying everywhere software driving hardware, coded living things, memories of inert and living objects, etc. *Totemist*, yes again, in all classifications: Linné, Lavoisier, Mendeleev. The behaviour of these inventors mimics that of Algonquins or Sioux, gathered around the Bear or the Eagle. Just as the Earth was formed by accretion, just as evolution formed my body by accretion, so it seems to me that I can envision an *accretion* of these four continents.

A composite metaphysics?

These variations do not indicate that the sciences require the complete absence of ideologies or sundry views, but on the contrary that they let float, around and in them, and compatible with them, an accretion, a pudding, a disparate composite, I was going to say a loam, a compost, a stem from which they spring; they emerge from all over. Gold veins abound in rocks thought to be sterile. We invent *at all costs*. Can we conceive the sum of it all?

To Leibniz, he again, the stem mind of God totals all elementary and disparate possibilities; in combining them, says the classical philosopher, he creates a differentiated infinity of worlds. The preface to *The Troubadour of Knowledge* attempted to translate this image for a humbler mind; it presented a Harlequin, wearing his usual cloak, polychrome, chequered, speckled, mixed, mottled, blended … a tattered patchwork of a thousand shapes and colours; supposing that these pixels are multiplied ad infinitum, the sum of these hues that we arrive at verges on white light in the end. Harlequin becomes Pierrot. There's the *white stem.*

Starting from a partial view, every person, every culture, finds a means of entry, a doorway to science, that does not destroy the singularities as such, individual or collective. Parthians, Medes, residents of Asia and Cappadocia … they each understand it in *their* language; every dialect, every view, opens an access to it; there is not one door only, but rather several, and all are oblique. The scientific debates and controversies that are often claimed to advance the history of science provide a source of pleasure to fundamentalists in ideologies and never actually oppose scientists for the sake of knowledge. The fierce battles between all manner of Michurinian Marxists, deterministic materialists, reductionists and creationists to which my short life has been exposed and from which it has not ceased to suffer never led to an invention and did nothing but oppose pugnacious individuals hell bent on fighting it out, just as, in the past, dogmatists of a given theological party disputed each other in public, often to the point of tragedy. No, a compact stem exists on the horizon of divergent views. Let us invent a new Irenicist – *Pacificus philalethia* – passionate about this compact truth.

If a stem metaphysics were to exist, then its totemist component would inspire classification methods; its animist component would stimulate evolutions and great stories; naturalist, it would establish a knowledge of objects by subject; analogist, it would never stop bridging extravagant differences with meticulous isologous combinations. This is the outcome of the book: have we any need for more?

As for Philippe Descola, the book's guide, look at him, the totemist, classifying; the animist, believing in interiority; the analogist, traversing all cultures; the naturalist, positing the universality of physicalities. Does he cultivate, in ethnology, a Catholic stem? No, science, simply ... a tale of anticipatory literature?

The ease with which continents with ever-changing cultures welcome science – Parthians, Medes, residents of Asia and Cappadocia ... let the gentiles in! – comes less from its truth or its applications than from its anthropological 'catholicism'. If each culture finds its unique value, this value must be there already. The world's universities function like parishes, with domineering archbishops, fat canons, virulent heretics and god-botherers persecuting mystical monks. The history of science runs parallel to the history of religions; what is called, here, with insistence, a paradigm shift is called, there, heresy or Reformation.

I specify again, to avoid any confusion, that there are relations and there is reason. If reality is rational, relations (*ratio*) saturate, subtend, and solidify it. But not everything is calculable; there is contingency. If reality is related, relational, religious, all sorts of connections (*re-ligare*) run through it. The second hypothesis, broader, vaguer, less dominated, indefinite even, includes the first, narrower, definite, rigorous, effective, mastered. Three crowns: the systems, rational and emerged, appear like rare islands; accreted, connected, numerous, they are surrounded by bricolages; a chaotic sea bathes them.

Christiane Frémont translated the literal sense of the expression *Catholic religion* by the totality (ὅλον, *olon*) of relations (*re-ligare*); in other words, the *universal of relations*. As for Philip Descola, once again, he says *relative universal*.

Freer still and sometimes a step ahead of the sciences, literature sometimes indulges in the same descriptions. Thus the chaos of forms and colours in Balzac's *The Unknown Masterpiece* lets the trace of a foot emerge – ἴχνος, *ichnos*, in Greek; the ichnography or the geometrical plan totals all profiles or perspectives, brought together here kaleidoscopically, and it detaches from them. Thus are displayed the three or four magnificent miscellanies of Flaubert: the divine accumulated jumble in *Temptation* and that of the altar over which Félicité dies designate a Catholic religion, in the aforementioned sense; as for that of *Bouvard and Pécuchet*, it seems to me to describe the current *Paysages des sciences* (Landscapes of the sciences). All evoke this *ideal stem*.

And I am one too! At the end of *Temptation*, Saint Anthony, delirious, becomes stem.

'– O happiness! happiness! I have seen the birth of life, I have seen the beginning of movement. The blood in my veins is beating so hard that it will burst them. I feel like flying, swimming, yelping, bellowing, howling. I'd like to have wings, a carapace, a rind, to breathe out smoke, wave my trunk, twist my body, divide myself up, to be inside everything, to drift away with odours, develop as plants do, flow like water, vibrate like sound, gleam like light, to curl myself up into every shape, to penetrate each atom, to get down to the depth of matter – to be matter!'

I *cogite* therefore I am a Saint Anthony.

Stanford, November 2008

Contents